THE MARY MYTH

THE
MARY MYTH

ON THE FEMININITY OF GOD

ANDREW M. GREELEY

A Crossroad Book
THE SEABURY PRESS · NEW YORK

For my two theology "professors"
David Tracy
John Shea

1977
The Seabury Press
815 Second Avenue
New York, N.Y. 10017

Printed in the United States of America

Second Printing

Library of Congress Cataloging In Publication Data
Greeley, Andrew M   1928–   The Mary myth.
"A Crossroad book."
1. Mary, Virgin—Theology.   2. Femininity of God.
I. Title.
BT613.G73   232.91   76-53545
ISBN 0-8164-0333-3

At morning's first misty light
They came out of the primal bogs
And worshiped in the holy woods.
They tended the sacred fire
And sang of the land of promise
  beyond the seas in the fabled west.

They told tales of heroines and gods
Sad Deirdre, mighty Finn
Noble Dermot, frenzied Maeve.
Then Podraig—
And soft as summer rain
A new and loving god
  came gently to their dreams.

Ah, great men they were—and women too
But it's all over, 'tis the end.
We shall not see their like again.

Bards and monks, scholars and saints
Bishops and kings, hermits and pilgrims
They printed the books and taught the schools
  and claimed they prayed the whole night long.
By the smoking peat the learned scholar
With weary eye and bobbing head read his sacred text;
And zealous Pangar Ban pursued the local mice
While Holy Brigid kept a great pool of ale
  for the welcoming of the King of Kings.

Doubtless brave and a little mad
They lit the lamps of Europe
Conquered the conquering Dane
  and then lit the lamps again
While Holy Brendan sailed to the land of promise in the west.

Insula sanctorum? Not always.
Still, great men they were—and women too
But it's all over, 'tis the end.
We shall not see their like again.

v

Through rocky fields they walked, down the muddy lanes
Past the empty cottage and by the youthful corpse
On to the leaky ships, across the mountain sea.
Sick, hungry, poor, afraid.
Into the slum, the tavern, the gutter
The mill, slaughterhouse, the early tomb.
Like Holy Brendan they sailed to the land of promise in the west
    and found hatred, misery, and sudden death.

Oh, yes, great men they were—and women too
But it's all over, 'tis the end.
We shall not see their like again.

Out of their neighborhoods they climbed
Onto "the cars," into "the force"
Teacher and priest, mayor and doctor
Lawyer and crook, nun and nurse
They sang, they danced, they talked the whole night long.
They cried at births, they laughed at wakes.
They drank, they talked, they fought
    and then they talked again.
And on dark gray autumn afternoons
    they prayed for the triumph of Notre Dame.

Indeed great men they were—and women too
But it's all over, 'tis the end.
We shall not see their like again.

So it is all over now.
And tears flow at the country club
For all the glories that were
And all the greatness that might have been.
We made it at last in the land of promise
And damn proud we are.
We showed them. We won; we got in.

It is the end of our tale
But what does it matter?
We glow briefly in the sun's lingering flame
As, martini glass in hand, for the final time
    we pray for the triumph of Notre Dame.

Ah, great men we are—and women too
But it's all over, 'tis the end.
They shall not see our like again.

So lean thinker and towering poet
What are you two doing here?
Have you not heard my sad refrain?
The tale is told, 'Tis over, finished, done.
Join the others at the wake
   and sing and drink to the end of it all.
Poet and wise man, druid and monk
Migrant and rebel, monsignor and cop
All dead and buried in the ground.

Today in the land of promise, can it be? Is it true?
Are there still some of us around?
Are there stories yet to be told?
A few mysteries still to be probed?
Songs to be sung, work to be done
   in the melting pot that didn't melt?
Not yet curtains for the crazy celt?

So, generous teachers and loyal friends,
The sun still rises over the misty bogs,
Not all that far from Scarsdale to Mayo
   or from Kerry to Oak Park.
Let it then be writ on the morning sky:

God help them all.
But it is not the end.
They shall indeed see our like again.

Andrew M. Greeley
June 21, 1976

A NOTE ABOUT THE ILLUSTRATIONS

The illustrations in this book are not merely decorations but are an integral part of the arguments:

——The five Christian images of Mary are more important indicators of Mary's role in the Christian tradition than any theological writing. All are women—even the ethereal Spanish girl painted by El Greco. All are sexual creatures, all represent sharply defined "feminine functions," all represent profound and powerful experiences of sexual differentiations as revelatory of the sacred. It is a pity that women were not encouraged to create their own marian art since then we would have, from both men and women, images of the Christian experience of femininity as revelatory of the sacred.

——The black and white pagan art is designed to show the structural and functional similarity between the experience of sexual differentiation as sacred in Christian and non-Christian religions. Thus both the Tibetan Tara and the Medieval ivory figure present the image of the "young girl as divine." The Michelangelo barrelhead madonna and the prehistoric Sardinian madonna both reflect the experience of woman as mother. The Egyptian Horus with her dead son parallels the Michelangelo pietà. And the modern pagan representation of the attractive goddess of love, Eriu, is roughly analogous to the virgin daughter of Zion whom Yahweh desired in the Botticelli *Annunciation.*

The contemporary Irish drawing is interesting because it represents a legendary Irish goddess in a mixture of modern advertising-poster art and ancient celtic decorative themes—but not completely free from some (perhaps unconscious) marian influence. The ancient Irish drawing from the burial passage at New Grange may depict the three different roles of women in prehistoric and preceltic art—mother at the beginning of life, spouse during the course of life, and death (pietà) at the end of life.

It has been wise, perhaps, to keep secret the fact that Ireland gets its name from an ancient celtic goddess of sexual love!

CONTENTS

Part I

PROLOGUE

OUR LADY'S DAY IN HARVEST TIME

The blue mantle hangs useless from the peg
Dust and darkness dim the window
Stale air presses heavy on the land
Summertime—and yet we are cold.

No passion in the empty house
No laughter in the shabby garden
No rapture in the frigid heart.

Long gone she who used to wear the sky—
Bright Brigid, sweet Astarte, gentle Net;
Long gone, too, bewitching teenage peasant
Who bore the world anew

Who tamed the Norman fury
Who warmed the Saxon soul
Who kept alive the Polish hope
And calmed the crackling Celt.

Worthless the mantle and brown her garden
For whom the whole world once sang
"Dei Mater Alma."

The generous belly, the breast soft and warm,
The merry eye, the tender hand—all long, long gone.

Now the icy ideologue, the ivory ikon,
The sickly cult, the papal text,
The dry debate, the dismal "no."

Where gone, Madonna, and how long?
Alive? Well, in what galaxy?
And we orphans, chilled and alone,
Among the rotting roses.

The wind shifts,
The mantle lifts,
White fingers on blue cloth,
Flashing brown eyes in the sudden sunlight,
A smile explodes against the gloom.
Laetare, Alleluia!

A.M.G.

Chapter 1

A RETURN TO MARY?*

T his is not a book about Mary; it is about the God who is
revealed to us through Mary. This is not a book about
women; it is about human nature as it is revealed to men
and women through the "masculine" and "feminine" dimensions of women.

It is, therefore, a book about hope. The God who is revealed to
us in Mary is a God who inspires hope; and in the reproductive
powers of the human race, in the fertility of the womb, humankind has experienced from the beginning the biological ground
of hopefulness: we may die but the species continues.

We go to Mary, then, to learn about God. We go to women,

---

* There are critics who will argue that only a woman should write about the
femininity of God. Such an argument is ideological romanticism. Only the young
should write about the young, only the nonwhite should write about the nonwhite, only Jews should write about Jews, only married people about marriage,
etc., etc? Such an ideology is also anti-intellectual, reactionary, and oppressive; I
will not dignify it with serious discussion. The question about any book ought
not to be what are the ascribed characteristics of the one who writes it but how
good it is. Men have at least as much interest in God being female as do
women—though perhaps their interest is from a different perspective. This book
is written from the male viewpoint because the writer is male. Presumably in
some of the man-hating, quasi-lesbian circles of "the movement," this will be
enough to make the book an exercise in chauvinism. Too bad for them. A woman
might have different insights into the femininity of God than a man; so much the
better. Fortunately humankind is blessed with the special insights and experiences of both sexes.

then, to learn about ourselves. I intend this volume to be an exercise in neither traditional mariology nor the contemporary feminism—though I do not deny the value of either. I assume all the titles and doctrines of the traditional mariology, and I assume all the critiques of contemporary feminism; but I write neither about new titles of Mary nor the old oppression of woman by man (or its converse). I write about the God revealed in Mary and the human nature revealed by woman, a God of hope and a people of hopefulness despite themselves.

Hope is currently in bad repute—mostly, I suspect, because it has been confused with naïve evolutionary optimism, an optimism which died in Europe on the bloody battlefields of 1917 and was buried in the Hiroshima explosion of 1945. In this country full realization of its death struck home in the assassination-riot-Vietnam-Watergate nightmare of the 1960s and early 1970s. Unable to distinguish between optimism and hope, many thoughtful Americans, disabused of their optimism, are giving up hope too.

Robert Heilbroner begins his immensely successful book, *An Inquiry into the Human Prospect*,[1] with a question he admits he would hesitate to ask aloud if he did not believe it existed unvoiced in the minds of many, "Is there hope for man?"

Will there be a future that has anything else but a continuation of darkness, cruelty, and disorder? Heilbroner says no. Does worse impend? Heilbroner responds yes. Part of the problem, he insists, is that we have discovered once again that man does not live by bread along. "Affluence does not buy morale, a sense of community, even a quiescent conformity. Instead, it may only permit larger numbers of people to express their existential unhappiness because they are no longer crushed by the burdens of the economic struggle."[2]

He concludes his melancholy but clear and painfully honest prognosis for the future of the liberal, secular, rational, democratic society (of which he is both product and interpreter) with a quest for a myth, a symbol around which we can rally our will to survive. The Promethean spirit has brought us trouble; perhaps from another figure in Greek mythology we can find peace.

With some sense of pride Heilbroner offers us the symbol of

Atlas, "bearing with endless perseverance the weight of the heavens in his hands." We must resolutely bear our burdens, we must preserve the very will to live, we must rescue the future from the angry condemnation of the present: "It is the example of Atlas, resolutely bearing his burden, that provides the strength we seek. If, within us, the spirit of Atlas falters, there perishes the determination to preserve humanity at all costs and any costs, forever." [3]

An Inquiry into the Human Prospect is a profoundly melancholy and depressing book, although I cannot help but admire Heilbroner's clear-eyed courage. Atlas, I suspect, is but a projection of the steely determination of Heilbroner's own spirit. Equally pessimistic books, though lacking Heilbroner's stoicism and self-discipline, have been written by Loren Eiseley (who suggested that the evolutionary process made a mistake when it produced humankind), Richard Goodwin, and Peter Schrag.[4] There is also the infamous *Meadows Report,** which turns out not to be much as either economics or computer science but is pretty effective apocalypse.

I wonder whether the wave of doom and gloom is merely the latest fashion among our intellectual and cultural elites. Is *An Inquiry into the Human Prospect* only a successor to *The Greening of America?* Charles Reich was a Pelagian who believed in the end-

* Dennis L. Meadows, et al, *The Limits to Growth.* New York: Universe Books, 1972. For a devastating critique of this book see H. S. D. Cole, ed., *Models of Doom: A Critique of The Limits to Growth.* New York: Universe Books, 1973. See in particular the response of the Meadows team on pages 239 and 240 of the book. The Sussex University critics have utterly destroyed the economic basis of the Meadows prophecy of doom. The MIT researchers take refuge in a response that is prophecy and apocalypse, indeed one might even characterize it as religion instead of economics.
This book is not an exercise in economic analysis; however I would note in passing that the enthusiasm of many religious leaders and spokesmen for zero economic growth has not persuaded me that it is either necessary or desirable. On the contrary, all the evidence I am aware of suggests that zero economic growth would be an unmitigated disaster for humankind. The notion that resources are limited is at best a half-truth and at worst a dangerous falsehood. Competent geologists, agriculturists, and biologists have repeatedly argued that while there may be problems with individual resources, there is no forseeable shortage of any basic raw material in the world. Unfortunately, these sane and sober men do not seem to capture the imaginations of religious leaders.

less perfectability of humankind (carried out by a messianic younger generation—made up mostly, it would seem, of Yale students). Heilbroner is a neo-Manichee struggling bravely in the face of doom. Will the late 70s see the pendulum swing back to the Pelagianism of Reich?

However, both Heilbroner and Reich share a common theme which I think represents a major shift in the thinking of intellectual leaders in the North Atlantic community. Both are engaged in apocalypse; both see the end of the world as we now know it; both have abandoned faith in the Enlightenment worldview; both see the failure of the liberal, rational, democratic ethic. Heilbroner also sees a failure of socialism as well as capitalism. Reich confidently expects rebirth, Heilbroner pessimistically expects doom; but both see the modern world as having come to an end. Reich rejoices, Heilbroner laments; but neither sees in the future a place for the easy rationalistic confidence of the Enlightenment.

And here we might mention a third contemporary prophet who mixes Heilbroner's pessimism with Reich's romanticism. The modern world, the world of the Enlightenment, has indeed come to and end for Theodore Roszak, and somewhere out beyond the wastelands the counterculture, equipped with *The Whole Earth Catalog* and other such resources, is beginning to build a new "gnostic" civilization. Roszak is less pessimistic than Heilbroner but not nearly so easily optimistic as Reich. For him, the square society is likely to limp on for a long time. Reich seeks salvation in Consciousness III; Roszak seeks it in the poetry of Blake, Wordsworth, and Goethe. The Meadows team wants to return to some kind of pre-Judeo-Christian state of nature (in which there would be no electricity for the computers). Heilbroner grimly takes the weight of the world on his shoulders and offers us the myth of Atlas as we bravely and patiently await our doom.

Well, maybe.

But as my colleague William McCready remarked to me, "Atlas is the name of a tire. Whoever built a cathedral to honor a tire or wrote a love poem in praise of one?"

At the turn of the century, a remarkable prescient American intellectual addressed himself to the same questions that torment our present intellectuals. Anticipating air fight, nuclear energy, and the computer before any of these wonders were invented, he asked what room there was for humankind in a world dominated by the dynamo:

> What are we then? The lords of space?
> The mastermind whose task You do?
> Jockey who rides You into space?
> Or are we atoms whirled apace
>   shaped and controlled by You?
>
> We are no beggars! What care we
> For hopes or terrors, love or hate?
> What for the universe? We see
>   only our certain destiny
> In the last word of fate.

Henry Adams, "The Virgin and the Dynamo"
from *Prayer to the Virgin of Chartes.*

It was not, however, to an obscure, unimportant Greek mythological figure that Henry Adams turned as a focus for his emotions in a response to the dynamo. He turned to another symbol of the Western culture:

> Simple as when I asked her aid before;
> Humble as when I prayed for grace in vain
> Seven hundred years ago; weak, weary, sore
> In heart and hope, I asked your help again.
>
> You who remember all, remember me;
> An English scholar of a Norman name,
> I was a thousand who then crossed sea
> To wrangle in the Paris schools for fame.
>
> When your Byzantine portal was still young
> I prayed there with my master Abelard;
> When Ave Maris Stella was first sung
> I helped to sing it here with St. Bernard.
>
> When Blanche set up your gorgeous Rose of France
> I stood among the servants of the queen;
> And when St. Louis made his penitence,
> I followed barefoot where the King had been.

> For centuries I brought you all my cares,
> And vexed you with the murmurs of a child;
> You heard the tedious burden of my prayers;
> you could not grant them, but at least you smiled.
>
> Henry Adams, *Prayer for the Virgin of Chartres.*

There is no way that the American intelligentsia as represented by such writers as Schrag, Goodwin, Meadows, and Heilbroner will turn to the smiling Virgin of Chartres. Even though they may have lost hope in their Enlightenment rationalism, they are still so much products of the Enlightenment that they could only smile in amusement at the thought that the smiling Virgin might have something pertinent to say to the modern world.

Still I wonder. The Marian symbol is surely one of the most powerful symbols in the Western tradition. Virtually every major painter from the fifth to the sixteenth century painted at least one Madonna. Great cathedrals sprang up all over Europe and still stand. Poets sing her praises, including such improbable characters as Petrarch, Boccaccio, Francois Villon, Shelley, Byron, Rilke. Football teams enter battle in her name. It will be a long time before a football team named after Atlas is number one. On the basis of history, if nothing else, in any competition between Heilbroner's Atlas and Henry Adams's Virgin of Chartres, there isn't much doubt who would win.

If Enlightenment rationalism is truly moribund—and the signs that it is are overwhelming—then we have entered into an era of the open marketplace for religious symbols. Heilbroner's push for a sustaining symbol in Atlas is merely the beginning of a search which is likely to occupy the North Atlantic world for a considerable time to come. Under such circumstances, the Mary symbol ought at least to be reconsidered on the possibility that a symbol which has had as much power for most of the history of the Western world as it did may still have some power of illumination in our time. It may be that our predecessors—not all of whom were howling savages—saw something in the Mary symbol that we have missed. What they saw might well be something we can ill afford to neglect.

There are signs that the reevaluation of the Mary myth has already begun. From his perspective out beyond the wastelands, Theodore Roszak remembered at least one thing from his Catholic background:

> The early and medieval Church remained pliable enough to accommodate to some degree the widespread need for myth. The major manifestation of this was the cult of the virgin, which elevated the inconsequential figure of Mary to a stupendous symbolic stature. Here was the mother goddess Christianity lacked, worked up out of the meagerest historical material by the mythic imagination—a triumph of collective visionary power at times so sweeping that the virgin nearly crowded out the official trinity. Of course, the theology of the church deftly delimited mariology; but that had little meaning at the level of popular worship or artistic creation, where the virgin rapidly occupied the psychic ground that had always been held by Isis, Cybele, Magna Mater, and their ageless sisterhood. After all, how poor and unbalanced a religion it is that does not find place for the Divine Mother.[5]

Lynn White, in his book *Machina Ex Deo*, comments: "The virgin mother, undefiled yet productive, bearing Christ into the world by the action of the Spirit of God, is so perfect an analogue of the most intimate experience of the soul that that powerful myth has sustained dubious history; for to the believer, myth and history have been one." [6]

Harvey Cox notes in his *Seduction of the Spirit:*

> Our overly spiritualized sentiments about immortality reveal yet another way in which our curious blend of technology and Victorianism has removed us from our own bodies. If pressed to a choice between symbols, I vastly prefer the Assumption to Ethical Culture. If God is dead, Mary is alive and well and she deserves our attention.[7]

He adds later, "I don't think we should overlook the fact that in some of her manifestations Mary is not just a woman but a powerful, maybe even a liberated woman." [8]

A Protestant writer is also prepared to contend that Protestantism has made a serious mistake in its opposition to the virgin:

> Ignoring the place of the Blessed Virgin in the Incarnation and the whole process of salvation has given Protestantism a harsh thoroughly masculine emphasis. . . . The absence [of tenderness and affection] in Protestantism has led to an over-emphasis on a harsh prophetic picture of God with its attending preoccupation with judgment. . . . The development of a mature Mariology in Protestant thinking could do much to temper the harsh portrayal of the God of judgment and provide it with a healthy (and I might add, scriptural) concept of a God of mercy.[9]

The research and thought out of which this book has grown began with two observations: the Mary symbol had overwhelming power for almost all of our predecessors, and a number of perceptive observers outside the Roman Catholic Church see value in the symbolism precisely at a time when Marian devotion seems virtually nonexistent among progressive Catholics. It seems that we had another example of what I modestly term "Greeley's Law:" non-Catholics start something the day after Catholics abandon it. I am not advocating a return to the Marian devotion of our Catholic childhoods; I am rather recommending a reevaluation of what the Mary symbolism really stands for on the grounds that Mary might be extremely relevant (to use a good if frequently abused word) for the problems of our time—at least as relevant as Atlas if not substantially more so. I began this investigation with no other predispositions. I am surely not trying to defend Mary, nor am I trying to rehabilitate her. (On the basis of the historical evidence, she needs neither defense nor rehabilitation.) I am certainly not trying to "apologize" in either sense of that word for traditional Catholic teaching. My Marian piety was nonexistent when this project began. The most I started with was a fascination with the history of the Mary myth and a hunch that there was more to be said about it than Cardinal Carberry's lugging the Fatima virgin around St. Louis.*

* The word "myth" is used in the title of this volume and throughout to mean a story which is a "mysterion," a "sacramentum," a revelation of a "Great Secret." Religious myths may or may not have a historical "referent." In the Jewish and Christian traditions, if myths are not grounded in historical events, they lose all value. To say, therefore, that the Mary story is a myth is not to say that it is a

I therefore propose in this book a reevaluation of Mary from the point of view of the social sciences, or at least from the point of view of a social scientist. I will contend that Mary is a symbol of the feminine component of the deity. She represents the human insight that the Ultimate is passionately tender, seductively attractive, irresistibly inspiring, and graciously healing. I will argue that the Mary symbol arises out of the human "limit-experience" of sexual differentiation and as such she can legitimately be called a "sex goddess." Mary is, in other words, part of a great tradition of female deities, all of whom reflect the human conviction that God has feminine as well as masculine characteristics, a conviction arising spontaneously and inevitably from the profound, disturbing, and shattering experience of sex differentiation.

Among the many excellent recent treatments of the subject of the role of myth in religion, one of the clearest is Ian Barbour's *Myths, Models, and Paradigms.* According to Barbour, myths offer ways of ordering experience, inform man about himself, express a saving power in human life, provide patterns for human actions, and are enacted in rituals (pages 21–22). Barbour observes (page 23) "In the Western religions myth is indeed tied primarily to historical events rather than to phenomena in nature. This difference is crucial for conceptions of history, time and ethics, but it need not lead us to deny the presence of myth in the Bible. Divine action is in itself no more directly observable in history than in primordial time or in nature."

Obviously such an approach to the Mary myth is different from most previous ones. I do not reject either the contribution or the validity of those approaches; I am adding a new one.

I hope at all costs to avoid the battle of the Reformation over Mary (one of the most unseemly and foolish conflicts in the entire history of Christendom). The antipathy of some of the re-

---

legend. It is a story rooted in historical events, which is a revelation of a Great Secret.

Some Christians are still uneasy when they hear this technical use of the word "myth." It is a good word with a precise and proper meaning, and one that lends itself to scholarly analysis. Christians should not be nervous about its use.

formers and their followers to Mary was a disastrous mistake, as were the Catholic superstitions which in part caused the antipathy and the triumphalism which followed. In the view I propose to develop in this book, it will be seen that the reformers were quite correct in insisting that Mary had taken on a quasi-divine role in the Catholic tradition. They were wrong, however, in thinking that such a role detracted from the worship of God; for we shall see that Mary, like all feminine deities, reflects a central component of the deity and does not detract from its fullness. On the other hand, I think Catholics apologists have made a serious mistake by denying the obvious connection between Mary and the goddesses of pagan antiquity. In their overanxious fear that Mary would lose her uniqueness, they lost a powerful weapon in the controversy with the reformers and also an insight which might have enabled them to make Mary a much more pertinent symbol to fill the religious need to see the deity as both masculine and feminine. In excluding the feminine component of the deity, the reformers, as Dickson remarked in the passage quoted above, missed a very important and indeed a well-nigh universal component of human religious experience. It may be that the perspective offered in this book will provide a context in which the last of the Reformation battles over Mary can be resolved. But I do not wish to pause overlong on what surely must be in our age an obsolete conflict.

Nor will I put much emphasis here on the specific Marian doctrines proclaimed or discussed by the Catholic Church. I surely do not deny such doctrines, and I think the paradigm that I will develop will be able to subsume them. However, my interest is not in specific doctrine but in religious symbolism, and I would contend that the doctrines may be best understood as theologically directed attempts to explicate the symbols (some attempts being more successful than others, no doubt).

I will not repeat in this book the work of contemporary Scripture scholars on the Marian passages in the New Testament. Such works are readily available and can be consulted by anyone who is interested.[10]

The four primary scriptural images of Mary—the New Eve, the Church, the daughter of Zion, and the Virgin—will fit into my paradigm. But much of the present controversy, in particular over the nativity narratives (important in its own right), is not pertinent to my basic purpose.

I have consulted the works on Mary by the great theologians of our time: the Rahners (Karl and Hugo), Schillebeeckx, Laurentin, Congar, Semelroth, and Thurian.[11] I fear that none of these books has been particularly helpful to my purpose; mostly, I suspect, because the theological method at work in them permitted the authors to take no serious consideration of the contribution to the study of the theology of Mary that might be made by the history of religions. Juniper Carol's three-volume *Mariology* series, Frank Sheed's *The Mary Book*, and Hilda Graef's Marian history have been useful for source material, but I fear the three authors would find my use of that source material surprising, to say the least.[12]

Since my approach emphasizes so heavily religious symbolism, I have leaned much more on poetry and art than has traditional theology. The best available collection of Marian verse is still Sister Therese's *I Sing of a Maiden;* two collections of art by Henri Gheon and one by Jean Guiton have been helpful to me.[13]

Just as I have no desire to contend with Protestants about Reformation controversies over Mary, I am resolved not to argue with the traditional Mariologists within Catholicism. I have cited some of the literature of that tradition to make it clear to critics who will arise from these quarters that I am not unaware of their work. I must say in all honesty that the high Mariology of the theologians is simply not very trenchant. And the popular Mariology seems bent on multiplying titles and miracles (where it survives at all) and is likely to turn off both Catholics and non-Catholics.*

I will confess to being most impatient with popular Mariology

---

* Perhaps the weakness of most of the current Catholic theology about Mary is that the authors are unwilling to take the step that the history of religions enables them to take and see Mary as a reflection of the femininity of God. Still, one theologian saw such a step over a half century ago. Pierre Teilhard de Chardin spoke of the "biopsychological necessity of the 'Marian' to counterbalance the masculinity of Yahweh." He argued that the cult of Mary corrects a "dreadfully masculinized conception of the godhead." [Quoted in Henri de Lubac, *The Eternal Feminine* (London: Collins, 1970) p. 125–6].

even in its present moribund state. It is creepy, and does a great disservice to Our Lady, who has been a prisoner of creeps far too long. I see little purpose in this book in spending time and energy arguing with those to whom no one listens.

My approach to the Mary myth combines elements of sociology, the history of religion, and some of the most recent developments in what might be broadly called "language" theology. My definition of religion and my notion of the role of religious symbols is based on the work of Clifford Geertz and Thomas Luckmann; I have developed this component of my research in my book, *Unsecular Man*.[14] For the material from the history of religions, I am indebted to Mircea Eliade and (with some reservations) to the Jungian, Erich Neumann.[15] The theological input comes chiefly from the work of Langdon Gilkey, Paul Ricoeur, Peter Berger, Nathan Scott, Thomas Fawcett, Ian Ramsey, and especially David Tracy.[16] The last-named writer has brilliantly synthesized much of the best in current theological thought. I am deeply in his debt.

In the following chapters I will attempt to show how I have combined these three different areas of religious thought into my own approach (I hesitate to use that overworked word "method") to religion. I am very carefully stating in the first two chapters both what I am doing and what I am not doing. I do this in order for the reader to have no doubt about my context, my perspective, and my purpose. The approach I have elected to use to better understand the Mary myth is new, perhaps startlingly so. Like everything new it runs the risk of being misunderstood. I take it for granted that many of the things I say will be eagerly snatched out of context and distorted by hostile reviewers. By carefully describing my sources and my approach and excluding questions which are not explicitly pertinent to that approach, I hope to minimize misunderstanding and distortion. There are many aspects of Marian devotion and Marian theory which I do not discuss in this book; it is not, therefore, to be concluded that I do not believe in these Marian doctrines or that I think they are unimportant. My concern in this book is not to repeat old approaches but to explore a new one. My approach should be judged not by whether it is true or false; it is an approach and not a statement. I would rather be judged on whether my approach is useful or not. Those who find it so are welcome to use it; the others are welcome to forget it.

Some readers of an earlier draft of this volume have questioned whether I am an "orthodox" Roman Catholic because I do not assert my belief that Mary is the "Mother of God." I must confess to mild annoyance about this propensity to hunt heresy (which I had thought went out with Vatican Council II). Just because someone does not *assert* his acceptance of a particular doctrine does not mean that he does not *accept* it. I cannot understand why it is necessary to go through a ritual of repeating all the doctrines one accepts so that one may be judged "orthodox" as preliminary to proceeding to the work at hand.

Of course I accept the *theotoxos* (*"mater dei"*) title. It has an honorable history of 1500 years, and no Catholic Christian could possibly reject it. I feel that I deal with it at great length in the Madonna chapter of the book. If I do not spend time on the explicit "Godbearer" title, the reason is that many modern readers can cope with it only if they understand the "communication of idioms" thesis of Christology. Without such understanding, the assertion that Mary is the Mother of God will not only be paradoxical (which, like all good limit-language, it ought to be) but incomprehensible. But to develop an explanation of the "communication of idioms" would take us into Christological problems beyond the scope of this book, as well as the competency of its author.

However, to say that Mary is "the mysterion," the *imago dei,* is not to give her a lesser title than *theotoxos* but a greater one. To put the matter differently, Mary is the *imago dei* because of her maternity. As Jesus himself said in response to praise of his mother, "Rather blessed are those who hear the word of God and keep it." In other words, blessed are those who reveal and reflect the goodness and love of God.

The thesis of this book, then, is that Mary reveals the tender, gentle, comforting, reassuring, "feminine" dimension of God. Surely such a thesis is so traditional as to be pedestrian.

Some commentators on earlier versions have also complained that I do not acknowledge that Mary is an object of faith in herself, and that I do not confess my faith in all the things we must believe about Mary. To make Mary the object of faith, I think, would be to fall guilty to what the Protestants have accused Catholics of doing for centuries. There is only one object of faith—God. All the "doctrines" we believe are about God. They all manifest God to us, reveal something of his nature, give us some hint of his love. This book is not about Mary. It is about God revealed to us through Mary. Those who are horrified by such a strange idea should read what St. Thomas has to say on the subject (II-II, 1, 1). One quotation should suffice for our present concerns: *"Objectum fidei is unun; non solum in actu quo credimus sed id quod credimus."* * The "quod," of course, is God.

The core of my approach to Mary is a paradigm, a four-celled "model" that represents four aspects of the Mary myth— Madonna, Sponsa, Virgo, and Pietà—which correspond to four elements of the human "limit-experience" of sexual differentiation. It is important to understand what a model is to a social scientist: it is a tool for examining reality, not a description of what reality is. Whatever elegance and symmetry there may be in an intellectual model is gained at the price of eliminating much of the complexity, diversity, the ambiguity and "messiness" of the world the way it really is. If one wishes to engage in generalization and abstract thought about the real world, one must schematize, divide, order, and organize the phenomena of experience. One must insert discontinuities where there is continuity, division where there is unity, clear definitions where there is in fact a steady flow of complex phenomena. A model, even the most elegant one—I might even say especially the most elegant one—is necessarily a distortion of reality because it is a simplification of reality.

There is no harm in any of this as long as one keeps in mind that the model is *not* reality. A real problem arises when any model-builder (or his disciples) begins to confuse the model with reality, and indeed identifies the model with reality so that the model becomes more real than the phenomena which it tries to subsume and organize. But we who are model-builders are much

---

* Translation: "The object of faith is one, not only the act by which we believe, but that which we believe."

like the little boy with his airplane; we are terribly proud of our creations. We are tempted to act as though the real world is an affront when it doesn't fit neatly into our elegant systems.

Thus the Freudian paradigm of id, ego, and superego is an extremely useful tool until we permit ourselves to think that there is actually out there somewhere a reality of the human personality, a segment or a force or a division which corresponds precisely to the notion of Freud's model. When we think about it, of course, it becomes clear that the human personality is much more complicated than the neat, tri-layered picture the Freudian theory presents, or the "collective unconscious" of the Jungians, or the binary models of Claude Levi-Strauss. They are all so attractive and elegant that it is easy to begin to think of them as precise descriptions. It is not evident that Freud, Jung, or Levi-Strauss failed on occasion to succumb to the temptation to view them as such; certainly many of their followers have done so.

I want to make clear from the very beginning that my model for the Mary myth is nothing more than a way of organizing data, a perspective from which one can view phenomena, a tool for a very good, sometimes at best, suggestive, and sometimes relatively weak, analysis. But it is an abstraction, a schematization, a simplification of a reality that is in every instance far more complex, elaborate, subtle, and indeterminate than my model. Those religiously inclined people who are used to apodictic certainties in their approach to religion will be appalled at the notion of a religious model as a perspective instead of an absolutely unchallengeable description. So be it. Reality, even religious reality, is far too tangled and fluid to be captured by apodictic certainties.

All models, then, are to some extent metaphors. Freud's three-layered self, Jung's collective unconscious, Levi-Strauss' binary world are all approximations; all say in effect, "The world is *like* . . ." Every model is in some sense a form of "limit-language"; it is designed to startle us into a perception that we did not have previously, to give us an insight that we hitherto lacked. Religious models, as we shall see, are limit-language par excellence. They differ from other models, it seems to me, in degree and not in kind. My four images of Mary are nothing more than an attempt to shatter our old perceptions of the Virgin symbolism and help us to see it in a new light.* If we then see Mary in a new light, she in turn becomes a model that shatters our perceptions of ultimate reality and helps us to see it in a new light. She guides us to see ultimate reality not only as creating, organizing, ordering, directing, planning, bringing to completion but also tenderly caring, seductively attracting, passionately inspiring, and gently healing. The purpose of this book is not to teach new doctrines or to deny old ones; it is merely to offer new perceptions, new insights, a new structuring of experience. If new language is used, the reason is that new language can produce, or perhaps renew, experiences. I invite the reader to judge this book on this criterion: Does it provide him with new or renewed experience of the illumination shed on the human condition by the smile of the Virgin in the way Henry Adams was renewed in the shadow of Chartes?

Two final comments: First of all, I am not merely asserting that the Mary myth is a useful way to propound the femininity of God in an era when feminism is strong. I am arguing that the structure and function of the Mary myth are designed to reveal the femininity of God. The theologians may have missed the point or have been afraid to touch it; but the poets and the painters have not—nor have the Christian faithful. My attempt,

---

* For purposes of clarification I perhaps should add that my fourfold paradigm is a "model about a model." For within the Mary myth itself there is a model (the "structure" of the myth, to use Barbour's phrase) which purports to tell us about God.

In the text I may go too far in the direction of what Barbour calls "instrumentalism," denying to a model any reality beyond its utility as a tool. Anyone interested in this not unimportant methodological distinction should consult Barbour (op. cit.). The model, he tells us, should be taken "seriously" but not "literally." Deductions from the theory to which the model leads must be carefully tested against the data. The model is a mental construct, not a reality; but the critical realist "tries to acknowledge both the creativity of man's mind and the existence of patterns in events not created by man's mind." We must grant the model some "provisional ontologic status," which means we believe that there are "entities in the world something like those described by the model . . . there is some isomorphism between the model and the real structures of the world" (p. 42). Still, the critical realist "makes only a tentative commitment to the existence of the entities something like those portrayed in the model" (p. 47).

then, is not to offer a new interpretation of the Mary myth but to make articulate and explicit the function of the myth from the beginning.

I am not a theologian. Yet I cannot pass this book off as sociology. It is an exercise in the margins between the two disciplines. Perhaps it is even theology done from a sociological perspective. In the past I have inveighed mightily against theologians who cross the boundaries of sociology without respect for sociological method; I am therefore conscious of the risk of making the same mistake in reverse. Hence I have turned to two theologians, David Tracy and John Shea, as an apprentice striving to learn and to respect the methods of their discipline (in this case, a method they both use). As I understand them, they tell me that I have not too egregiously violated the rules of theological methodology. I am grateful for the education in theology I have received from them (hence the manic Celtic dedication of the book to them), but like all other teachers, they should be dispensed from responsibility for their students' errors.

I experienced renewal in the writing of this book. My devotion to Mary was almost nonexistent. There is now a statue of Mary in my garden. The next thing I need is flowers. In the meantime, I turn to the substance of the book with the prayers of that incorrigible sinner, François Villon.

> Lady of Heaven and earth, and therewithal
>   Crowned Empress of the nether clefts of Hell,—
> I, thy poor Christian, on thy name do call
>   Commending me to thee, with thee to dwell,
>   Albeit in nought I be commendable.
> But all mine undeserving may not mar
> Such mercies as thy sovereign mercies are;
>   Without the which (as true words testify
> No soul can reach thy Heaven so fair and far.
> Even in this faith I choose to live and die.
>
> O excellent Virgin Princess! Thou didst bear
>   King Jesus, the most excellent comforter,
> Who even of this our weakness craved a share
>   And for our sake stooped to us from on high,

Offering to death His young life sweet and fair.
Such as He is, Our Lord, I Him declare,
  And in this faith I choose to live and die.

François Villon (1431–1485), *His Mother's Service to Our Lady*,
translated by Dante Gabriel Rossetti from the French.

Chapter 2

RELIGION, EXPERIENCE, SYMBOLS, LANGUAGE

We moderns think of religion as creed, code, and cult. It is a series of propositions to be believed in, a set of moral practices to be followed, a body of ritual to be observed. A man's religiousness is measured by his denominational attendance, his church affiliation, his acceptance of certain doctrinal propositions, his adherence to certain moral norms, and his performance of certain approved rituals. It is all very neat, orderly, and rational. If the sociology of religion has generally not progressed beyond the measurement of such phenomena, the reason is that most sociologists of religion, like most of the rest of us, are very much products of the Enlightenment, and see religion as essentially propositional.[1]

In fact, however, such a rationalistic view of religion describes neither what religion has meant to people in the past nor what it means to most people today. Religion is humankind's way of wrestling with the ultimate; it is the set of answers, usually in nonpropositional form, to the most fundamental and basic questions a human has about the purpose of life and of the world in which he finds himself. Indeed, religion is an explanation of what things are all about. Creed, code, cult, church are all derivatives; they flow from the basic worldview, the fundamental interpretive scheme. They are important, indeed, but decidedly secondary to the intuition of the real, which is the primal and revelatory religious phenomenon. Clifford Geertz provides a useful definition of religion from this perspective. Religion is:

(1) a system of symbols which acts to
(2) establish powerful, pervasive, and long-lasting moods and motivations in men by
(3) formulating conceptions of a general order of existence and
(4) clothing these conceptions with such an aura of factuality that
(5) the moods and motivations seem uniquely realistic.[2]

Religion, then, is a symbolic interpretation of ultimate reality that provides templates, guideposts, road maps according to which people can chart their way through the oobscurities of life, particularly as these obscurities are manifested in the most ultimate questions of purpose and meaning that a human can ask himself.

But why does religion appear in symbols before it appears in closed propositions of catechisms and theology books? At one level the answer is simply that when one deals with the most primal or the most ultimate, prose is not enough. The proposition appeals mostly to the intellect; the symbol appeals to the total personality—will and emotions, as well as intellect. But more must be said. Religion appears first of all in symbols, in dense, complex, multilayered, polyvalent pictures, stories, rituals, because religion takes its origin from experience, and religious communication is primarily designed to lead to the replication of experience.

The Enlightenment witticism of Voltaire that man creates God in his own image and likeness, has been repeated often. God, the Ultimate (or whatever we choose to call it), was a product of man's dreams, his self-deception, his wish fulfillment; but it could be more accurately said that man creates himself in the image and likeness of the God he experiences. Religion takes its origin in experience, and humankind shapes its life in the context of the view of ultimate reality it derives from its experience. Religious symbols are not merely a way of passing on the basic truths that one individual or a group learn from a religious experience which gave rise to their religious faith; symbols are in fact designed to recreate the experience itself, to produce in the one who views the symbol a religious experience like that which led to the creation of the symbol.

But what kind of experiences produce religious symbols? They need not be the ecstatic variety described by such different authors as William James and Abraham Maslow. Such experiences are far more common even in our modern "secular" world than many people had thought. (Approximately two-fifths of the American public has had such extremely intense ecstatic experiences.[3]) Ecstasy is not required for a religious experience. Basic issues arise implicitly or explicitly, consciously or unconsciously, whenever we brush up against the stone wall that creates the boundary lines of our existence. When we push up against our own finite limits we find ourselves wondering what human life means, and in that experience of finitude we obtain a hint of an explanation, a fleeting glimpse of an answer.

The scientist wonders whither come the imperatives that move him to work and discipline his efforts. The ethicians wonder why we have an overriding sense of moral obligation. Lovers locked in passionate embrace, the mother wiping away the tears of her child, a tired and weary pilgrim refreshed by a clear spring morning, light breaking through the clouds, a parent or a spouse dies, a friendship ends in bitter quarreling, one fails, one realizes that one is old, one knows suddenly that one will die—all these are or can be, in Father David Tracy's words, "limit-experiences." The scientist knows that his science cannot measure the imperatives that set him to work; they are beyond the limits of his knowledge. The ethician knows that his ethics can never reveal their source. The lovers understand that however strong the passion that unites them, they are still two separate persons, and both are doomed to die; the mother perceives that these tears she can wipe away but that there will be others to fall later in life that no one will be able to wipe away. We cannot always help those we love and there will come a time when they will not be able to help us. Life is finite, and within the boundaries of life our own particular existence is hemmed in on all sides by physiological, biological, psychological, and sociological limitations.

We may be pilgrims of the absolute, we may hunger for the infinite; but the being that we experience in our daily lives is all too fragile, all too finite.

And yet . . . and yet . . . In such experiences of limitation we also may experience something more. The limit can become a horizon that not only defines where we are but also suggests that there is something beyond where we are. In the limit-experience we bump up against the wall that imposes a boundary on our finite existence; but then, perhaps only for a fraction of a second, we find ourselves wondering why the wall is there, how we exist in relation to the wall. Is there something or perhaps even some-*one* else on the other side? And every once in a while, in such horizon- or boundary-experiences, we have the impression that perhaps the wall moved a bit, or maybe we heard someone whispering on the other side of it.

I am not suggesting that limit-experiences are a "proof," as the old logical, rational arguments were. We do not argue that the limit may be a horizon, the boundary a disclosure; we rather sense it intuitively as a briefly glimpsed possibility.

The power of the limit-experience to "disclose" reality to us is in its power to stir up wonder. For we sense not merely the limitations on our existence but the gratuity, the giftedness of that existence. And if existence is gratuitous and gifted, then it may also be gracious. And if there is graciousness, from whence does it come? The limit-experience, then, is a "religious experience" precisely in its capacity to stir up wonder in us about grace. The scientists and the ethicians wonder about the imperatives that preside over their disciplines, the mother wonders about the marvel that is her child, the two lovers wonder how such great joy as is theirs can possibly be. Faced with the limitations on human affection and friendship, we wonder how friendship can be possible at all; and finally, pressed up against the wall of death we are still baffled by the phenomenon of life and by the refusal of life to give up hope even when we can see no farther than the wall of death.

The horizon-experience, then, is a revelation. It does not provide an "answer" to the agonized problems that our limitations impose upon us; it is a revelation in the sense that it is a "hint of an explanation"; it offers us a fleeting glimpse of the possibility of grace; it gives us a hint, sometimes subtle, almost imperceptible, and at other times powerful, that there is "something else" going on in our lives, and if there is, there may also be "something else" beyond the horizon. Religion, necessarily and inevitably, is about that "something else."

Such experiences are "rumors of angels," "signals of the transcendent," or, in David Tracy's more metaphysical words, "disclosive of a final, a fundamental, meaningfulness [which] bears a religious character."

These "disclosive" experiences reveal to us a world of meaning beyond the everyday, and this world is that through which religious symbols come. One might even say that it is a world out of which religious symbols explode. As Tracy notes: "Such a 'world,' by its strange ability to put us in touch with what we believe to be a final, a 'trustworthy,' meaning to our lives may also disclose to us, however hesitantly, the character of that ultimate horizon of meaning which religious persons call 'gracious,' 'eventful,' 'faith-full,' 'revelatory.' " [4]

Limit-situations and limit-questions pose the fundamental religious issues, and, on occasion at least, they also suggest what the answers might be. Our thrust for self-transcendence—in scientific search, in moral and philosophical reflection, in celebration, in service, in love—runs up against Something Else (or Someone Else) which is perceived as having set boundaries to self-transcendence; and more than that, this Something Else is also perceived as responsible for both the self and the thrust for transcendence; or, alternately, it is the object of our longing for transcendence. It is perceived as having set a limit which is not permanent, as having created a stone wall which may eventually tumble down, as having drawn a boundary line, but a temporary one—or, to anticipate the theme of this book, it is perceived as a seductive lover, teasing us to go only so far but seeming also to promise that she (he) may be willing to give even more.

In the limit-experience one experiences oneself as thrust into being, and one wonders about Being: Which is the ground, the origin, the goal of such a thrust? To be thrust into being is gratuitous. We did not ask for it; it was simply given. We wonder, therefore, about the nature of Being. Whence comes this gift? (It is possible, incidentally, to be technically a philosophical atheist and still state the question in this fashion. Martin Heidegger,* who taught us to ask the question in this way, denies that Being is the same as God. He describes himself philosophically as an atheist.)

It follows, therefore, that anything that shares in Being, any being, can be the occasion of a limit-experience. Any being can be revelatory of Being. There was a time when our simple ancestors saw the whole world animated by spirits—a tree, a rock, a wind, a star were all revelations of the sacred reality because each of them was animated, inhabited by some sort of spirit. Nathan Scott observed that in the animistic frame of reference, everything was sacramental, at least potentially, because everything was capable of revealing the sacred world, the real world at work behind the ordinary events and phenomena of daily life. Some things could be sacraments because everything was sacramental; some realities could be especially holy, especially revelatory, because all reality was fundamentally holy and revelatory. Scott also argues, rightly I believe, that even if one abandons—as modern humans must—the animistic worldview, one can still see the whole of reality as sacramental. If one accepts the idea that all beings are revelatory in Being because all beings participate in Being, grace—in the sense of the revelation of the given-ness of our existence—comes from some sacraments, because everything is potentially sacramental. Grace is everywhere, or, as Karl Rahner says, "everything is grace."

There are, of course, certain human experiences with a special capacity for revelation, but they have this special capacity because everything has potential for revelation. Some things are especially sacred because everything is primordially sacred. As the poet Richard Wilbur puts it:

* There is a charming and true story about Heidegger, a sometime Jesuit seminarian, in his old age arranging flowers in a country church for the celebration of the anniversary of a Jesuit relative. The old philosopher genuflected each time he passed the tabernacle. A curial official present for the festivities turned to a distinguished theologian who had studied under Heidegger and asked, "But why does Heidegger genuflect? Isn't he an atheist?" To which came the ironic reply, "A rationalist like you wouldn't understand."

. . . Oh maculate, cracked, askew,
Gay-pocked and potsherd world
I voyage, where in every tangible tree
I see afloat among the leaves, all calm and curled,
The Cheshire smile which sets me fearfully free.

Richard Wilbur, "Objects" [5]

I will argue in this book that sexual differentiation is sacramental in the sense that it has an extraordinarily powerful potentiality for creating in us a boundary or limit-experience, an experience in which the harsh wall of our own finitude is almost
brutally encountered but which is also an experience of the revelation of the possibility of graciousness beyond the wall.

Two things must be noted about sexual differentiation as sacrament: Like all other sacraments, it need not be sacramental.
While it has the capacity of inducing limit-experience, sexual differentiation need not do so, and most of our experiences of sexual differences are not very clearly or very explicitly limit-experiences. Secondly, sexual differentiation is sacramental because
the whole material world is sacramental. Sexual differentiation
can reveal to us both the limits of our own quest for transcendence and the hint of a possibility of breaking beyond those
limits precisely because it participates in the mystery of a universe that in both its totality and its individual parts imposes
limits to and poses questions about the possibility of transcend-
ing the universe itself.

What does it take for a thing to be a sacrament, for an object or
a person to become a revelation, for an experience of a thing to
become a disclosure? As Thomas Fawcett remarks, "A disclosure
of any kind is only possible when something within a man's experience confronts him in such a way that a response is evoked
within him." [6] When a thing becomes a disclosure, it also becomes a symbol. Trees, flowers, tiny animals are simply things;
but when they are carried in a spring procession, they become a
sign that spring has come. Even this really isn't a disclosure until
the signs "produce specific reactions in us, [until] they operate at
the personal level of emotion and imagination [and] something
new appears to be given in the experience they create." [7] The

flowers, the tree branches, the animals are not merely a sign that spring is back, they have become a disclosure sign precisely because they create in us an experience of bumping up against the limits of the cosmos. The signs which announce spring speak of both death and life; the world is not dead, it constantly overcomes death. I see that sign; it forces me to consider my own death and discloses to me in one way or another that death is not ultimate. The thing has become a sign, and the sign in its turn, because it has evoked tough questioning and a tentative answer in me, has become a symbol.

Note well what has happened. The thing which has forced a limit-experience on me now becomes the symbol by which I interpret my experience and communicate it to others. This transformation of a thing into a limit-experience and a revelatory experience occurs, according to Fawcett, in three moments:

  (i) The presence of an existential need.
  (ii) The moment of disclosure or perception itself.
  (iii) The embodiment of the experience in symbolic form.[8]

The existential need has to be there to begin with. There has to be some predisposition toward a limit-experience before the thing can produce such an experience. I can see the dune grass turn green every year and just remark to myself, "Well, it's spring again." Unless there is some need in a particular spring in the depths of my personality to wonder about the mysteries of life and death in the universe, the second and third steps of the limit-experience may not occur. I can encounter a beautiful woman on the street and experience nothing else than a slightly increased level of sexual fantasy unless there is some kind of powerful existential puzzling going on inside of me about the diversity of humankind and the baffling differentiation of that kind into male and female, a differentiation combined with an urge toward unity between male and female. Without the predisposition to wonder, all things, even the most exciting things, become commonplace. But when the predisposition to wonder is there, then everything is potentially sacramental, and some things are overwhelmingly so.

Fawcett sees two phases in the process of a thing becoming a sacrament (my phrase, not his):

The Descent
  i. The presence of an existential need;
  ii. The moment of disclosure or perception of need;
  iii. The symbolization of ontological anxiety.

The Ascent
  i. The descent becomes the basis for further disclosure;
  i. Creative disclosure or perception;
  iii. Symbolizations of integration and wholeness.[9]

So I sit on the side of my dune with a need in the depths of my spirit (mostly unrecognized) to find some answer to the apparent chaos and absurdity of a human life that will surely be snuffed out in death. I then perceive that the dune grass is becoming green again; the grass is being reborn after a winter's death. "My God," I say (more in exclamation than in prayer). "The grass is reborn." It grows older without weakening, without becoming infirm. I too am growing older, but unlike the grass I move inevitably toward death. I have now symbolized my own ontological anxiety about death.

But I continue to stare at the grass. It seemed to be dead last November, but now it is alive again. Can it be that I am less important than the flowers of the field or the grass of the dune? I perceive that somehow, some way, life is stronger than death, that my life is stronger than my death. And so I celebrate the rebirth of the grass, the coming of spring, with a new sense of peace and serenity and wholeness. Life conquers death, and my life will ultimately conquer my death. Thus the symbol is transformed into limit-experience.

Or I encounter an extraordinarily beautiful woman. She is human like me but separate from me, distinct from me, not identifiable with me. I have been lonely, cut off, alienated, but have scarcely noted any existential need for union. In the experience of this beautiful woman, I perceive my alienation, my loneliness. It matters not whether I sleep with her. (The first person pronoun is used here in the general sense, *not* in any autobiographic sense.)

Even if we do make love, the moment of union with her is fleeting, and I perceive in it that I really am not "at one" with her, that I am distinct, lonely, cut off. My ontological anxiety has now been symbolized in my relationship with that woman, and in its explicitness I am forced to probe more deeply into the dilemma of loneliness. But I also perceive that in the differentiation that comes from our separateness and distinctiveness, there is also goodness, for she is tender and seductive and inspiring and gentle. She draws me out of myself both physiologically and psychologically. She discloses to me, and I perceive, that differentiation is a prelude to loving integration, and that which is separated can also be joined. If I feel cut off from myself, my friends, my world, from the ultimate forces that are at work in the universe, this woman becomes a sacrament to me that such divisions and separations and isolations can be transcended, and that differentiation is a prelude to wholeness.

Note that this experience of sexual differentiation can arise out of any encounter with a member of the opposite sex as long as there is a predisposing (perhaps unrecognized) existential need. The encounter can be the permanent relationship of a marriage or a chance passing on the street in which not a word is said. Note also that the experience of sexual differentiation, which is as commonplace as breathing, need not be sacramental. Sexual differentiation need not become a symbol; that it frequently has done so is beyond all doubt; that most of the time it does not become so in our lives is also beyond all doubt. Sex is not automatically a sacrament, but a lesson of human history is that it can easily become so.

What has happened in these two sacramental experiences? I have dealt with reality through an habitual structure of perceptions.* In my structured perceptions, dune grass and lovely women are parts of the environment, attractive and appealing in their own ways, doubtless, but quite ordinary and commonplace.

* The French philosopher Merleau-Ponty notes that humans organize and structure their experience simply because it is impossible to deal with an unstructured flow of consciousness. Such a structuring is a biological trait we have in common with the higher animals, though there is in humans, of course, in addition to the unconscious, biological structuring of experience, a conscious, reflective structuring. However, this latter builds on the former, which underpins and supports it.

But in a particular encounter in which these things * become sacramental, a peculiar dialectic is set up between my existential needs and the revelatory power of the thing. Thus, between my yearnings for self-transcendence and the thing's unique and special capacity to reveal Being, the dialectic is established that reveals the pain of the limit-experience, consciously and explicitly hints that something beyond the experience may be perceived, and transforms the thing itself into symbol which embodies both my perception of the problem and my grasp of the hint of an answer.

Because of the dialectic that is set up, the ordinary structures of my perception have been shattered. The grass is no longer a green flora on my duneside; it rises in revolt, as it were, against such casual, structured perception and demands to be seen for what it is, a wondrous, marvelous splash of green which some playful spirit has tossed on my dune, perhaps as compensation for last year's erosion. "Look at me!" the grass screams. "See what I am! Learn from me about the Being which I reveal." The grass, then, shatters the structures of my perception and becomes a symbol which is a focus, a prism through which my perceptions are restructured. The grass serves three roles: it shatters my old perceptions, but only once I have agreed implicitly to the establishment of the dialectic; it reorganizes my perceptions into a new configuration; and it accompanies me as a symbol which will recall for me the experience I had on the dunes and enable me—if I am a poet—to share that experience with others.

Similarly, the woman also virtually screams at me (when my existential needs force me to be open to dialogue with her): "I am not merely part of the environment. I'm not part of the scenery. I am a person like you, but different. I am cut off and lonely like you, and in the difference between us lies the possibility of unity. In that unity we have together is the union of all things in whatever is ultimate." The woman, then, forces me to recognize my own "cut-offness"; she becomes a revelation of the potential unity of all things, and in that moment becomes a symbol—a symbol that does not cease to be a human person, of course. She

---

* To call a beautiful woman a "thing" is not male chauvinism, merely an assertion that she shares the physical universe with me.

remains a symbol around which I can organize my newly restructured perceptions of unity and diversity, of alienation and love. As a symbol, my relationship is not fleeting; she recalls to me my limit-experience of isolation and a hint of an explanation about unity which responded to that limit-experience. She not only has restructured my perceptions, she is a permanent reminder of that restructuring, and hence a guarantee that I will not slip back. Finally, should I be a poet or a novelist or a musician, she is a symbol through which I can communicate to others my limit-experience and the dazzling insight that comes from the shattering of old perceptions and the creations of new structures.*

A limit-experience is essentially an experience of old perceptions being shattered and new ones being structured. It requires a dialogue between my existential need and the revelatory power of something else that shares the cosmos with me. At the core of the experience is the symbolization of that with which I am in dialogue. When, therefore, I speak to others of my experience, I necessarily fall back on the symbol because in one very real sense, the symbol *is* the experience.

Note that the symbolization of the thing, which is at the core of a limit-experience, is action-producing. I do not sit and look at the grass passively after it has intruded itself sacramentally into my life. I set out to work with a song on my lips (Well, I would if I could sing!) and joy in my heart. Restructured perceptions lead to restructured living. One lives in response to the world one perceives; if one perceives the world differently, one lives differently. When I fall in love with a woman who reveals to me the existence of passionate tenderness in the cosmos, my behavior undergoes a transformation. I yearn to be with her, I sing about her, I praise her to all I know. If she is already mine and I am already hers, I desperately wish to make love with her precisely because of my experience of her as a valid and authentic "other," I experience a powerful yearning for unity. She has restructured my perceptions, and in the process she has inevitably changed my behavior.

* All of this, of course, is highly schematic. It leaves out that when our sacramental encounters are with other people there is a necessary dialogue of respect for the other person's limit-experiences which may be going on simultaneously.

We act, therefore, as a result of limit-experiences. The apostles experienced the risen Jesus, and then went forth and preached him. The nature lover sings, the lover makes love. The apostles preached for years before they wrote about it, and only then did they begin to turn to theology. One reflects on the symbol and its meaning only after one has lived—perhaps passionately—the renewed life the symbols have made possible. Reflection is derivative; action is primary. Reflection focuses on both the symbol and the subsequent action, and tries to explain to others— especially those to whom the symbol is not an effective means of communication—what the experience incarnated in the symbol and embodied in one's life really means.

There is a unity in human religious experience simply because a number of things which are almost inevitably sacramental is finite. The sky, sun, moon, waters, stones, trees, the rebirth of nature in spring, special places and times, sexual differentiation, fertility, the life cycle—these are sacraments in virtually every culture the world has ever known. Eliade, in his *Patterns of Comparative Religion,* suggests a universality of sacraments is simply the result of general structures of human existence. Each of those sacramental things are important for all humans by the very fact that they are humans. Thus one does not need to have to postulate anything quite so elaborate as the primal archetypes of the collective unconscious of the Jungians.

If there is a fundamental similarity of religious experience, there is also a great plasticity and diversity in the way in which the various "supersacraments" might be encountered and interpreted. The rebirth of spring (my dune grass) can be greeted by gentle, restrained processions or by wild orgies; one can respond to sexual differentiation as limit-experience in ways as different as the smiling Virgin of Chartres is from temple prostitution. There are primal symbols in the sense that certain things in the world have almost universally overwhelming sacramental power, but these primal symbols can take very different forms as they become the carriers of different specific religious limit-experiences, and as specific religious insights have grown out of these experiences. Everyone experiences the rebirth of spring a little differently. The great religious leaders and founders have their immense influence precisely because their experience of the sacramental things which are available to all of us are profoundly new and original, and because the power with which they elaborate the symbol of their limit-experience calls forth similar new or renewed experiences and insights in their followers.

Mary is part of the universal human experience of sexual differentiation as a sacrament of alienation and dealienation, of diversity and unity, of the combination of opposites in the one. Mary reveals, as do all goddesses, the feminine aspect of the deity. We do not see the same kind of deity in Mary that we do in Astarte or Kali, for example. The basic experience of shattering and restructuring of perception is the same in any experience of sexual differentiation, but the way the structures are shattered and the new organization that is imposed upon them by our encounter with the particular symbol (whether we are the first to encounter it or whether we encounter it through others) can be very different. The Mary symbol reorganizes, restructures our perceptions in a very different way than does the Kali symbol. Both reveal to us the combination of masculinity and feminity in the deity, but that which is revealed about the deity and that which is integrated into our personalities by the symbol is very, very different in the Mary experience than that which is revealed and integrated in the Kali experience.

Furthermore, even a specified limit-experience symbol like my encounter with the woman on the street, or the early Christians' encounter with Mary, is not a neat, orderly, unambiguous, simple reality. The thing which reveals itself to us reveals itself in its fullness; it is dense, multilayered, polyvalent. It says many things to us simultaneously, some of them surely paradoxical, some of them even contradictory. One who has fallen in love knows full well that no set of logical propositions is adequate to describe the complexity, the paradox of the beloved. One tries to say everything at once and ends up babbling. All things are complicated, and those things which are most likely to be sacramental are especially so. The best we can do when we leave off simply repeating the symbol and attempting to take just one aspect of the symbol to describe it, is to risk distorting the symbol substantially by neglecting its other aspects. I describe the seriousness and intelligence of my "mythical" loved one, but having done that, I may make her sound terribly dull because I have not had an opportunity to simultaneously describe her humor and playfulness.

So it is with limit-experiences and the language we use to describe them. It is not merely that such language is "odd," as Ian Ramsey says. If one is speaking of limit-experience, one must use special language simply because limit-experiences are different from the ordinary experiences for which ordinary language is appropriate. You don't describe an event in which a thing becomes a symbol in ordinary prose; you must fall back on metaphor, parable, paradox; you must introduce a "qualifier," as Ramsey says, which indicates to the listener or the reader that you are now using words in their limit-sense and not in their ordinary sense.

Of its nature limit-language involves tension. The two terms of the metaphor which is latent in limit-language must be in some tension if they are to produce the startling and perception-shattering experience in the listener which religious language is designed to produce. Such statements as "The first shall be last, the last shall be first." "He is dead but has risen." "She is a mother but a virgin." represent limit-language use of words—words used to convey limit-experiences. Paul Ricoeur says that the language we use to describe the limit-experience, which a symbol both created and attempts to repeat, goes to the limits of language. The language of religion does not so much deny the ordinary as it intensifies it. In Father Tracy's words, it is "an intensification of the everyday." The unexpected happens; a strange world of meaning is projected which challenges, jars, disorients our everyday vision precisely by both showing us the limits to the everyday and projecting the limit character of the whole." [10]

Limit-language, then, is designed to convey a limit-experience, to convert a thing into a symbol. It is language designed to make the symbol "explode with a linguistic power that discloses possibilities for human existence which seem and are beyond the limit of what our ordinary language and experience might imagine." [11]

Such writers as Dominick Crossen and David Tracy have

shown that the very language of the Gospel parables has been designed to establish tension, to cut through existing structures of perception with the sharp knife of paradox. There is tension built into, for example, . . . the juxtaposition of the words "good" and "Samaritan," or "first" and "last," which, even before we hear the stories, catch us by surprise and set us to wondering. Both in their substance and in their language the parables are paradoxical, shattering, exploding, and disclosing narratives. Every child, and the child in every one of us, is ready to plead, "Tell me a story." For the role of stories is to explain life, and the good stories, in their very substance and in the structure of their language become revelation. In the shattering, disturbing, confusing, and challenging parables of the Gospel we are confronted with "one possible mode of being in the world: to live with explicit faith, with complete trust, with unqualified love." The story asks us to consider the possibility that we can live a life of fundamental trust, confidence, and total commitment to the goodness which has exploded out of the story and is seeking to take possession of us.

Thus, attempts to persuade us to perceive a thing as a symbol results in necessarily odd, unusual, and apparently bizarre language. The explanation of symbols cannot be made to fit the dimensions of ordinary discourse precisely because it is concerned with shattering forms and structures of everyday perceptions and the discourse that may flow from it. But symbols and the language that attempts to describe them are ambiguous in a second sense also.

When a thing becomes a symbol, it speaks to us all at once, and much of what it has to say we hear very dimly indeed. When we describe our experience to someone else, when we attempt to produce in him the same shattering and restructuring of perceptions that occurred in our experience, when we try to turn the thing into a symbol for him, it is altogether possible that the experience which is produced in him will enable him to see something in the symbol that we did not see. Suppose I write a poem about my dune grass. I have not heard clearly everything the grass has to say, but if my poem produces a similar experience in someone who reads it, he may not hear everything I have heard but he may well hear something clearly but dimly perceived by me; and he may also hear something that was really there when the grass spoke to me, but which I missed completely. In reading my poem, he searches not so much, or at least not entirely, for the meaning behind my words, which I have designed to convey the kind of experience the grass produced in me. He also, and perhaps more importantly, is trying to find the meaning "in front" of the words; that is, what does the grass say to him when it has produced in him through the mediation of my words an experience similar to mine of a thing becoming a symbol. For example, I may not have noticed at all that thin, apparently weak roots of the dune grass indeed hold my great and mighty dune together, and if it were not for the grass, wind and rain and snow would wreak havoc with my dune (assuming the lake waves should leave it alone). Like me, the reader of my imaginary poem experiences the limit-situation of the death and rebirth of nature, but he also experiences an aspect of that rebirth which is truly there but which I may have only dimly perceived or missed completely—the powerful binding force of a reborn nature which holds the potentially disintegrating inanimate reality together. (And, of course, he thereby perceives all kinds of ecological implications of my experience, which I either missed or only vaguely sensed.)

Mind you, he is not distorting my experience; he is not reading into it something that is not there; he is having the same experience I did (or one very similar) through the mediation of my words. But he is perceiving something deep and latent in the ontological reality of the experience that I missed.

Similarly, I may know a woman for years and suddenly discover an aspect of her personality that hitherto had been shrouded in mystery. Indeed, if I am not constantly discovering new things about her, our life together has become dull and routine. It is not that I am reading something into our experience together that was not there; nor is it that she suddenly becomes someone she was not before. This aspect of her selfhood was always there and was always speaking to me, but our dialogue has only today developed to such a stage that I perceive her speaking to me about this aspect of her personality. I am not "getting behind" the meaning of our original experience of each other; rather, I am now "in front of" that experience and seeing in it something I never saw before.

It is a phenomenon something like this that Paul Ricouer has in mind when he speaks of the "prospective" sense of a text. When one searches for the "prospective" meaning of a symbol, one does not ask merely or even principally what he who first articulated that symbol within a specific religious tradition perceived consciously or explicitly; one asks, rather, what illumination we are able to receive from experiencing the thing-turned-symbol or the problem of being-in-the-world as we experience them given our situation, our information, and our insights today? If we permit the thing-turned-symbol to shatter our perspectives as it shattered the perspectives of its author, and then go on to reorganize our perspectives, what new structures of perception emerge for us? Can the limit-experience that he produces in us through the language by which he describes his experience give us illumination from the thing-turned-symbol that he missed, dimly perceived, or, in fact, couldn't perceive within the context of the time and place of his experience?

Metaphors, symbols, myths are open-ended. No limits can be set, notes Ian Barbour, to how far the comparison in such a figure of speech can be extended, because it has an unspecifiable number of potentialities for articulation left for the hearer or the reader to explore. "It is not an illustration of an idea already explicitly spelled out, but a suggestive invitation to the discovery of further similarities" (p. 14). It is precisely because a symbol (like a parable) is open-ended that it can be extended to new situations. The symbol presents a comparison to be explored, insights to be discovered, a many-faceted flow of images to be enjoyed. It illumines one's situation so that one sees aspects of reality which one might otherwise have missed; and at the same time the contact with a newly illumined reality can reflect back on the symbol itself and enable one to discover a potential extension of the basic comparison that was hitherto unperceived.

If a symbol were merely a logical proposition, the possibility of our finding new illumination in it would be nil; but the symbol is an experience and a record of an experience; and experience, as we have said before, is complex, dense, multilayered, and polyvalent. Another man's symbol may produce in us experiential insights that it did not produce in him without doing violence either to his experience or to the symbol which enabled him to share it with us. Obviously we must be careful that the experience is indeed the same or fundamentally similar to his. A symbol is not an inkblot into which we read our own preconceptions and needs independently of its own objective integrity. He who claims to have experienced, in an encounter with a symbol, revelations that are exactly the opposite of the insights of the author and of the insights of a long tradition of those in a community which shared the experience with the author, ought to seriously question whether it is the same symbol and the same tradition of which he claims to be a part. He who encounters the risen Jesus, for example, and announces bravely that in his encounter he has learned that death conquers life, has not had an experience which shares any historical, psychological, or existential continuity with that of any Christians from the apostles to the present. It may be an interesting experience but it is not a Christian one; and it is not the same experience or even a fundamentally similar one to that of the apostles on Easter.

Still, with the caveat that the symbol is not an inkblot and that we must respect the validity and the authenticity of the author's personal experience and of those who are part of the tradition the author began, it is still possible for us to receive illuminations from the thing-turned-symbol that were but dimly perceived or not perceived at all by those who first experienced it.

It is possible, I should think, that as theological discussion of Ricouer's "prospective sense" develops, a way will be found out of many of the knotty problems that cling to the development of doctrine which has plagued Christianity for centuries. However, such solutions will only be possible for those who carefully put themselves into the context of the theological approach being described in this chapter, and who refrain from quick judgments about the meaning of symbols.

Symbols do not "compete" within a religious tradition. They do not so much describe different limit-experiences as they describe different aspects of the same primal Great Experience.

There may be a "core" symbol or a "privileged" symbol, but the others are reflections of it, not its competitors.

The "privileged" center of a symbol system is not diminished by the existence of other symbols organized around it. The central symbol of Christianity is conveyed in the paradox "Jesus who was crucified is risen." Exactly the same passionately loving, passionately renewing God is revealed by the symbol embodied in the paradox of the "virgin Daughter of Zion who gave birth to the new Adam." There is obviously no competition between the two, and while the former is "privileged," it is necessarily contained in the latter—as it is in every other symbol of the Christian system.

From the point of view of the logic of religious language, the Reformation argument about honor to Mary detracting from honor to Jesus is absurd (which is not to say that all the reformers' objections to some forms of Marian devotion were absurd). There is no need at all to limit God's exuberant graciousness by insisting on only one religious symbol as being fully legitimate for a tradition. This book happens to be about the great experience of Christianity as it is reflected in the Mary myth. As I have indicated in an earlier book, *The Jesus Myth,* Jesus died and risen is the "privileged" symbol. God, not being a Calvinist, permits us, indeed encourages us (if the history of religions is any proof) to have other symbols which reflect the core symbol.

Both limit-experiences and those things which are most disposed to become the symbols that trigger and incarnate such experiences are in themselves radically neutral. One can encounter a grace, a sense of given-ness, or one can encounter absurdity. The existential need may be resolved by a reordering of perceptions into a new and more gracious constellation, or the need may be frozen into the old structures of perception which become bravely and stoically accepted in the face of an impulse, an urge toward a new structure. John Shea in his *Challenge of Jesus* (Thomas More Press, 1975) shows ingeniously how a tree—one of the universal things-that-may-become-symbol—was a sign of graciousness for Avery Dulles and a sign of despair for Jean Paul Sartre. What one does with a thing-becoming-symbol is shaped to a considerable extent by one's culture, one's personality, one's biography. I would maintain that there is a strain toward graciousness in a limit-experience, but it is one that can be resisted.

Schubert Ogden is surely correct when he suggests that there is built into the structure of our personalities an assurance of the fundamental purposiveness of our existence. The limit-experience can produce a symbol that "re-presents" that assurance, but one is free to reject an assurance of purposiveness as wish fulfillment and self-deception. Such rejection means a denial of a powerful thrust of our personality, but it can be and has been done—often.

In this book I intend to ask what illumination we can receive for the problems of our time by permitting ourselves the limit-experience of the thing-called-sexual-differentiation becoming the revelatory symbol that is incarnated in the Mary tradition. More simply, what we can learn for our own time by encountering Mary; what we can learn by permitting ourselves the same experience (or a fundamentally similar one) of the Madonna, the Virgo, the Sponsa, and the Pietà which other Christians have been experiencing for ninteen centuries. One must be faithful to their experience, but one must also be faithful to oneself and the situation in which one finds oneself in the world. Tracy describes theology as ". . . reflection upon the meanings present in our common human experience and the meanings present in the Christian tradition . . ." [12] It is precisely because the shape of our common human experiences changes through time—though always maintaining a continuity with the past, of course—that we can find richer and fuller and more illuminating meaning in our reflection upon the Christian tradition.

I have repeatedly referred to a symbol producing in us the same or a fundamentally similar experience which the author of the thing-turned-symbol had when in the dialectic of encounter his perceptions were shattered and restructured into new and better configurations. There is a problem here. No man can have the exact experience of another. Peter's experience of the risen Jesus was not John's; and neither of their experiences was exactly the same as the one that knocked Paul from his horse on the route to Damascus. My experience is not yours, neither of ours is Henry Adams's; and we three twentieth-century Americans do not have exactly the same experience as did St. Bernard.

But what does it take for the experience of the risen Jesus or of Mary to be "fundamentally similar" through time and space? To my knowledge no one has addressed himself to this problem, although there is an obvious common-sense answer to it. There were clearly differences in personality and "existential need" in Peter, John and Paul, you, me, Henry Adams and St. Bernard. It was obviously the same Jesus, for example, that both apostles encountered; and who would question that there was any fundamental difference between Bernard's Virgin of Chartres and the one Henry Adams encountered? The real problem arises when one gets to borderline cases.

I would submit that the question comes down finally to the new configurations of perception that emerge from a limit-experience. When the thing-turned-symbol shatters the old routines and habits with which I view the world, and reorganizes the raw materials of my perceptions into a new pattern, is there a "fit?" It need be only rough and approximate, of course, but the fit between my constellation of perceptions and those to be found among those who have had similar encounters from the beginning must be apparent. My personality is indeed different than St. Bernard's; the world in which I live is different. It would be unthinkable for there not to be very considerable differences between my experience of Mary and his. He emphasized aspects which I think are unimportant; I will emphasize elements which he but dimly perceived and others of which he could not possibly have thought. But allowing for these differences of personality and environment, is my response like Bernard's? Is it a response of enthusiasm and joy to an Ultimate which is perceived as passionately tender? I think that it is, and that I can, therefore, claim continuity with Bernard. There is a "fit" between my reordered structures of perception and his. We may sing different songs to the Virgin, but it is the same Virgin who tells us both of God's loving graciousness.

One more point must be made about the symbol that both creates a transforming limit-experience and incarnates the memory of that experience so we can share it with others. The symbol almost always appears in the form of a story, which we made oblique reference to earlier with a quotation from Tracy's book discussing the Gospel parables. The age-old cry of the child, "Tell me a story," is in fact a primal cry of the human race. We find ourselves caught in the middle of a story—like a movie that we began to watch in the middle. We don't know how or why the story of humankind began, and we don't know how it will end for either the species or for us as individuals. The transforming symbol purports to tell us about the beginning and the ending, and by so doing it shatters our old perceptual structures and orders new ones into new configurations. But the thing-becoming-symbol can enter the dialectic between our existential needs and our perceptions, not as a sort of disembodied figure floating around timeless like a Platonic Idea or a Weberian Ideal Type. The thing becomes a symbol precisely insofar as it manages to embody itself in story, an image rooted in our perception of our reality. The parables of Jesus have the impact they do precisely because in them the language of symbol, limit-language, appears in story form. They begin as all good stories must with the words, "Once upon a time . . ."

Like "Once upon a time a decree went forth from Caesar Augustus . . ."

At the heart of the limit-experience is a sensation of "given-ness," of "gifted-ness," or, to use the old word, "grace." The scientist discovers that the intelligibility of the universe is a given; it is *there*, and whence it came his science knows not. It is a gift, utterly astonishing and gratuitous. The philosopher finds a common human moral faith (infinitely varied in its applications, no doubt, but still common in its basic norms). Such a faith—the underlying premise of all moral discussion—is as gratuitous as is the intelligibility of the universe. Thus, in the limit-experience one not only bumps up against the hard outer boundaries, the horizon of one's own understanding and experience, one also encounters (or can encounter) something that appears to be a grace or a gift lurking on the boundary which suggests something else—a giver, perhaps—beyond the boundary.

It is when a thing is perceived as a gift, as a grace, that it can shatter our perceptual structures and begin to build new ones. When I beheld in my astonishment the marvelous gratuity in the being of my dune grass, then I found myself facing the apparent graciousness of a Being which (or who) thrust the grass into its being. Similarly, the attractiveness of someone who is sexually differentiated from me becomes a symbol—a thing-turned-sacrament—precisely when I begin to wonder about the utter gratuity of that differentiation. She becomes grace when it dawns on me that there is no particular reason why such a marvel had to exist; the fact of her existence—particularly of her existence for me—is a sheer gift, pure grace. She is *there*, no longer now as merely a lovely part of the scenery, but a mysterious gift *to me*, a gift to which I had no right and which didn't have to be. She remains herself, of course, but now she is a sign of mystery, a rumor of angels, a grace-bestowing sacrament.

When grace floods into my personality through such an experience, the old structures of perception are not only shattered, they are swept away. Since I now see the thing differently, as *given*, I now see everything differently. Such a limit-experience need not happen, of course. The grass can remain a sign of the return of spring and not invade my consciousness as a sign of grace and a symbol of resurrection. Similarly, the woman may remain a mere thing; she may even become a thing-that-is, a self like my self, yet still not a thing-turned-sacrament, a self perceived as sheer gift. In most cases, the grass and the woman will *not* become signs of grace, and the giftedness of things will not be noticed. But the point is that they *can* become signs of grace and hence can be transformed into symbols.

Obviously I am using the words "grace" and "sacrament" in somewhat different senses than they were used in the old catechism and theology manuals. "Grace" here means the capacity of a reality to possess our perception with the utter gratuity, the sheer given-ness of its existence. "Sacrament" is a thing-becoming-symbol which reveals to us its graciousness and the graciousness of Being in which it is rooted and from which it has been thrust into a being of its own. I would contend, by the way, that this use of the words is primary, and the old catechetical and apologetic use of them was derivative.[13]

In summary, then, religion is a set of symbols growing out of limit-experiences in which we bump up against the boundaries of our horizon but also perceive that there may be something beyond those boundaries. In a limit-experience—at least in one in which we receive a "hint of an explanation"—a thing becomes a sacrament, a revelatory symbol which dialogues with our own existential need, shatters the old structures of our perception, and gives us new insights by reordering and renewing our perceptions into new structures. The thing-turned-symbol constructs the new configurations of perceptions which move us to action, provides us with a memory of the past experience to sustain us in action, and also becomes a means of communication by which we can share our experience with others. Religious preaching and teaching is essentially the art of trying to induce in others the same limit-experiences that we have had and that the founders of our religious tradition have had.

All things are potentially sacramental. All have the capability of converting themselves from things to symbols. There are certain things, including sexual differentiation, which have special sacramental power. Their overwhelming importance in the human condition has made them sacraments in almost every major human religious tradition. These universal symbols, however, take on many different specific forms, depending on the experience of the specific religious tradition. Even within a context of a given tradition, different humans at different times and places will experience different illumination from the fundamentally similar religious experience generated by the symbol.

The language with which we describe our limit-experience and the symbols which cause and preserve them is necessarily odd or special language, language which startles, jolts, reveals, stirs up expectations and hopes. Language which conveys a symbol is like the symbol itself: it intensifies the ordinary and everyday, and opens up new possibilities for our life in the world.

In the "method" or the "approach" that I have laid out in this chapter, there is immense possibility for preaching and religious education. It is not a possibility that I think will be seized in the near future; it will require hard work, constant rethinking, and the abandonment of many old emphases and techniques. I am convinced, however, that the "method" is an excellent one for dealing not only with secularist unbelievers but also with faithful parishioners. In my own experience, it is much less offensive to traditional Catholics than some of the bizarre techniques of religious education currently being practiced in American Catholicism.

In any event, I now propose to apply this method to the limit-experience of sexual differentiation and to Mary, the most dazzling symbol of the transforming power of that experience. Even the moody early Victorian William Wordsworth, could not escape the dazzling power of Mary's charm:

> Mother! whose virgin bosom was uncrost
> With the least shade of thought to sin allied;
> Woman! above all women glorified,
> Our tainted nature's solitary boast;
> Purer than foam on central ocean tost;
> Brighter than eastern skies at daybreak strewn
> With fancied roses, than the unblemished moon
> Before her wane begins on heaven's blue coast;
> Thy Image falls to earth. Yet some, I ween,
> Not unforgiven the suppliant knee might bend,
> As to a visible Power, in which did blend
> All that was mixed and reconciled in Thee
> Of mother's love with maiden purity
> Of high with low, celestial with terrene!

> William Wordsworth (1770–1850) "Sonnet to the Virgin"

Chapter 3

THE ANDROGYNY
OF GOD

There is a story about a white male chauvinist racist who presented himself at the gates of heaven and demanded admission. A suspiciously dusky looking angel told him that there was just no way he could get in. The new immigrant wanted to know why, and he was informed that God didn't like him. Since he had been a pious Presbyterian all his life, the man was astonished. "Why doesn't God like me?" he asked.

" 'Cause God, she's black!"

The story is intended to be ironic, of course. We all know that God is an elderly white male with a long beard.

But in fact God is both masculine and feminine, and may well have been thought of as a woman long before she/he was ever thought of as male.

Primitive humans were convinced that all attributes existed as one in the divinity, and that therefore there was every reason to think that both sexes should be more or less clearly expressed together.[1] Eliade comments:

> Divine androgyny is simply a primitive formula for the divine biunity; mythological or religious thought, before expressing this concept of the divine two-in-oneness in metaphysical terms or the theological terms (the revealed and the unrevealed) expressed it first in the biological terms of bisexuality.[2]

49

The fertility deities are generally either hermaphrodites or female one year and male the next. The vegetation deities (Adis, Adonis, Dionysius) are bisexual. In Australia, with its very primitive aboriginal religion, the primal god is androgynous, just as he is in the most highly developed religions such as may be found in India. Siva-Kali are sometimes represented in the Indian religion as a unity. The Tantric Indian mysticism is designed to identify the initiate with the "divine pair" by making him androgynous.[3]

As ultimate reality and absolute power, God simply cannot be limited by any attribute whatsoever. Egyptian, Greek, Scandinavian, Iranian, and even Chinese gods were either expressly androgynous or carried residues of their more ancient androgynous condition. The emergence of divine couples (Saturn and Juno, for example) are in most cases later fabrications or reformulations of primeval androgyny. There are, as Eliade comments, innumerable cases of divinity being addressed as "Father and Mother." [4]

Alan Watts traces the theme of the primordial pair in his book *The Two Hands of God* by way of the Yin and Yang themes in Chinese philosophy.[5] He quotes one Chinese text that gives the explicitly sexual connotation of the Yang-Yin unity: "One Yang and one Yin, that is the fundamental principle. The passionate unity of Yin and Yang in the copulation of husband and wife is the eternal rule of the universe. If heaven and earth did not mingle, whence would all things receive life?" [6]

In a more recent work, *The Two and the One*, Mircea Eliade adds that in several of the Midrashic writings, Adam was androgynous: "Adam and Eve were made back to back out of a joint at the shoulder; then God divided them with an ax-stroke, cutting them in two." [7] Another Midrashic writer argued that the "first man was a man on the left side, a woman on the right." This slipped into Christianity through two variants of the Gnostic sect. For Simon Magnus, the primordial spirit was male-female, and the Essenes thought of the "celestial man," Adamas, as a male-female; and therefore Adam, a celestial "reflection" of Adamas, also had to be androgynous.

Plato viewed the archetypical man as bisexual and spherical in form, and his neoplatonic disciples (some of them Christian) imagined human perfection as an unbroken unity. Such philosophical speculations were rooted in earlier mythological convictions. The goddess Hera, the goddess of marriage, was originally androgynous; there are statues of a bearded Zeus with six breasts; in some cults Hercules was dressed as a woman. In Cyprus, Aphrodite had a beard, and in Italy, Venus was bald. Dionysius was addressed as a man-woman; he started out as a stout bearded fellow, though later he became much more effeminate. The sober Romans, never ones to take a chance, hedged when they addressed the deity: "Whether you are a man or whether you are a woman . . ." or "Whether you are a god or a goddess . . ."

Enough evidence has been produced to make the point. Eliade even sees some traces of this androgynous theme in the writings of early Christianity. In the Gospel of Thomas, for example, Jesus is quoted as saying, "When you make male and female into a single one, so that the male shall not be male and the female shall not be female, then you shall enter the kingdom." [8] Elsewhere in the same apocryphal Gospel, Jesus is pictured as saying, "When you make the two become one, you will become the son of man, and if you say 'Mountain, remove yourself,' it will remove itself." [9] In the Gospel of Philip the division of the sexes—Eve being made from the body of Adam—is the principle of death: "Christ came to reestablish what was thus divided in the beginning and to reunite the two. Those who died because they were in separation, He will restore to life by reuniting them!" [10] In the somewhat more reliable Second Epistle of Clement, Jesus is asked at what moment the kingdom will come, and he replies, "When the two shall be one, the outside like the inside, the male with the female neither male nor female." [11] Clement of Alexandria records the response of Jesus to Salome (in the Gospel according to the Egyptians) when that exotic dancer wondered about the fulfillment of the prophecy. He answered in terms she would doubtless understand, "When you have trampled on the garment of shame, and when the two become one, and the male with the female is neither male nor female." [12]

These apocryphal Gospels are either quasi-Gnostic or have

strong Gnostic influences, but Eliade sees some influence of the same perspective in the famous quote in the third chapter of the Epistle to the Galatians, "There is neither Jew nor Greek, there is neither slave nor free, there is neither male nor female; for we are all one in Christ Jesus." Against the background of the other texts, it seems by no means impossible that Paul's choice of words and phrases, if nothing else, was influenced by the androgynous speculation that was rife in his time.

The theme continued to be played in a minor key in Catholic theology through Maximus the Confessor, John Scotus Origina, and Nicholas of Cusa. Origina thought of God as a primal unity; the division of substances began with God and continued progressively up to and including human nature, which was divided into male and female. This division was the result of sin, but it will come to an end with the forgiveness of sin. Male and female will be reunited, and the circle will then begin to turn back to the primal unity of God. The reintegration is anticipated in Christ. Maximus the Confessor even suggests that though Jesus was born and died a man, in his risen state he was neither man nor woman. [13]

Nicholas of Cusa operated on a much higher level of abstraction. God was the *coincidenta oppositorum,* the combination of opposites—a notion Cusa probably picked up from the pseudo-Dionysius. Indeed, according to Nicholas, *coincidenta oppositorum* is the least imperfect definition of God.

Eliade sees this theme of the combination of opposites running through theology, metaphysical speculation, mythical cosmologies, orgiastic rituals in which behavior is reversed and values confused (the Saturnalia, the Mardi Gras, the Carnivale), mystical techniques for the union of contraries, and in rites of androgynization:

> One can say that all these myths, rites, and beliefs have the aim of reminding men that the ultimate reality, the sacred, the divine, defies all possibilities of rational comprehension; that the *grund* can only be grasped as a mystery or paradox . . . The best way of apprehending God or the ultimate reality is to cease, if only for a few seconds, considering and

imagining divinity in terms of immediate experience; such
an experience could only perceive fragments and tensions.[14]

The ultimate reality, then, is a primal unity. Creation represents a fragmentation of unity; reintegration involves putting the
fragments back together again. The Pauline notion of "restoring
all things in Christ" surely shows the influence of this primal
religious theme.

To many who have not made a detailed study of ancient or
primitive religious myths much of the material I have cited above
may seem bizarre. The statues on Hindu temples which show
male and female copulations in an incredible variety of different
positions strike us as being nothing more than pornography in
stone. Obscene they may be, deliberately erotic they surely are;
but they also reflect the almost universal human notion that in
God the masculine and feminine are blended in unbroken unity.
However startling and odd the androgynous themes may be, we
must admit that the scholastic philosophy in which we were
raised taught us that all human perfection exists in an infinitely
superior way in the deity. If masculinity and femininity are per-
fections, then they must exist in God—so the scholastic could
argue (in infinitely superior fashion, no doubt). Therefore, no
matter how strange we find the androgyny myths, we must
admit that even though we never heard of it in school, the notion
of an androgynous deity is certainly not incompatible with the
religious perspectives in which we were raised.*

* Merlin Stone, in *When God was a Woman* (Dial Press, 1976), argues that God
was feminine before becoming masculine, and that in the primordial food-gathering societies, matriarchy antedated patriarchy. Only later did the masculine god
enter as a secondary and lesser consort of the Queen of Heaven. Still later did he
expel the goddess from the divine court and set up a patriarchal and eventually
chauvinist society. Obviously the most chauvinistic of the male gods was Yahweh, who got rid of his consort and imposed terrible oppression on women.
Stone's book is a useful review of the literature on the female deities, but the
data will not support her model. Indeed, most sweeping evolutionary models of
human change go far beyond the existing evidence. The more we know about
primitive peoples (modern or ancient) the more difficult it becomes to fit specific
tribes into an evolutionary paradigm. Surely there is no real evidence to support
the old notion (first advanced more than 100 years ago by Bachofen in his *Mud-
derech*) that humankind has evolved from matriarchy to patriarchy. The reality

When we are forced to think of it, we must admit that God is neither male nor female. To put the matter differently, in God that which is most attractive in maleness and that which is most attractive in femaleness are combined in a higher unity. It is certainly proper, then, to think of God as he/she or she/he. The cautious Romans with their *"Sive Deus, sive Dea"* were theologically precise. For convenience sake, we have chosen for the most part to address God as male; however, there is no reason either philosophically or religiously why one could not, for convenience sake, make exactly the opposite decision and, following the ex-

---

seems to be that matrilineal (inheritance through women), matrilocal (living with mother's family), and matriarchal (women in governing roles) customs coexist at the same time and in varying patterns with one another and with patrilineal, patrilocal, and patriarchal customs; and that there is no great correlation between these customs and religious convictions. Thus the Celts and the Romans both had mother goddesses but women had far more freedom (virtual parity in many respects) in Celtic society than in Roman. Similarly Hebrew society had no (official) female deity but in practice Hebrew women seem to have had more power and more rights than did Roman women.

The research challenge is not to describe general models (many of which smack of female chauvinist ideology) but to ask under what circumstances one can find specifically a link between religion and social customs. Yahweh had no consorts (officially, at any rate—popular devotion to the Queen of Heaven obviously continued in Hebrew folk religion), but Yahweh also had many feminine characteristics—tenderness, warmth, and attractiveness.

Stone says not a word about the reappearance of the Queen of Heaven in the guise of Mary—which makes one wonder about how ideology can blind a writer. We do not have enough historical monographic work to detail the relationship between the slow improvement of the lot of women under Christianity (in comparison with the Hellenistic world) and the Mary cult, though there seems to be little reason to doubt the connection. However, correlations can run in either direction. It may well be that the more elevated role of women in Christianity ("neither Jew nor Gentile, male nor female, but all one in Christ Jesus") made possible the rise of the Mary cult.

Men are in a position to dominate women because they tend to be physically stronger and (apparently) more aggressive. Also women are at a special disadvantage during the child-bearing and nursing years. The extent to which this domination of the weaker by the stronger is a direct correlate of religious belief is a matter for research and not for theoretical or ideological assumption. But the presence of a female deity does not necessarily impede such domination—as the Graeco-Roman world makes clear.

Still, in one sense the thesis of Stone is undeniable. When God is completely lacking in feminine traits, as is the God of some Calvinists, there will be hard times for all weaker creatures—women, children, black slaves, American Indians, and Irish natives, among others.

ample of Juliana of Norwich address God as "Our loving Mother." My argument is not that one must or should address God as female; simply that one may.[15]

The feminine goddesses of antiquity, then, represent the fact that the "feminine principle" is present in the deity. They are developments from more primitive androgynous deities, in all likelihood, and of course they reflect the human experience of sexuality as sacred. Fertility is a good, indeed an indispensable thing, and fertility involves sexuality; then surely sexuality must be found in the ultimate and the absolute. But it is difficult to deal with an ultimate that is masculine and feminine at the same time. Therefore, we have gods and goddesses, and underlying the vast systems of ritual and cult we build to those deities there is still the notion that in whatever is *really* ultimate, the two are combined.

Indeed, if anything, the female deities, or the female divine forces, seem to have emerged before the male ones. There is one major difficulty, of course, in trying to get at the religious behavior and beliefs of prehistoric peoples; and that is that they were prehistoric. The data from which archeologists, physical anthropologists, and prehistorians work is at best very uneven and ambiguous. I am astonished at the elaborate and complex theories these scholars can build up with the kind of data which, if it were available to a sociologist, might well lead him to throw it in the wastebasket. I intend no criticism of these hardworking, creative, and sometimes extremely ingenious men and women; they have no choice; they must do the best with what they have. Still, they and we must be very cautious about accepting their theories.

It is undoubtedly the case that a substantial number of female figurines have been found in caves all over Europe, the Middle East, and Asia. It is very *likely* the case that these figurines have religious and cultic significance, but we do not know for sure since none of us was around to see what our cave-dwelling ancestors did with their figurines. The argument that the grossly shaped bodies of the statues indicate an abstraction which could only reflect some sort of religious purpose is persuasive, although I wonder if archeologists tens of thousands of years from now might not argue from an uncovered cache of *Playboy* center-folds that these were clearly religious artifacts.

Similarly, there were certainly strong matriarchal themes and social structures to be found in many archaic societies. In such societies it is also true that the mother goddess was more impor-tant than the father god: but it does not necessarily follow that matriarchy represented a peaceful and loving stage in human cul-tural evolution that was replaced by an aggressive, warlike patri-archal culture and social structure. Johann Jacob Bachofen's famous work, *Das Mutterrecht*,[16] is an extraordinarily ingenious organization of the data which cannot be ignored by anyone in-terested in the study of the history of religions. It is not, how-ever, a description of what actually happened historically in the sense that a Woodward and Bernstein article in the *Washington Post* is. The occasional writer (frequently feminist) who assumes that an evolution from matriarchy to patriarchy is a certainly es-tablished historical phenomenon (one that ought to be reversed) shows no awareness of the complexity and the ambiguity of the data of prehistory. In fact, patriarchy and matriarchy are en-twined, combined, and follow one another in bewildering pat-terns. They are "ideal types" and not simple stages of the evolu-tionary ladder.

I make these qualifications because I think it important for the reader to understand that a good deal of the data available to us about ancient religion is still very complex and obscure.

With all these qualifications it is still true that in the Paleolithic Age there seems to have been an intense devotion to the Great Mother goddess: "With the Stone Age sculptures of the Great Mother as a goddess, the Archetypical Feminine suddenly bursts upon the world of men in overwhelming wholeness and perfec-tion. Aside from the cave paintings, these figures of the Great Goddess are the earliest cult works and the works of art known to us." [17]

One may wonder about the "archetype" to which Neumann's Jungian ideology commits him. One may also wonder after look-ing at those rather grotesque figures like the Venus of Willendorf, the Venus of Menton, the Venus of Lespugue, and the Venus of

Laussel (see Plates 1 and 2 of the Neumann book) if they are all that "whole" or "perfect." The modern observer may consider them to be rather ugly, though on second thought he may reflect that they are, after all, not that different from a Picasso drawing. Indeed, with some modification, the Venus of Lespugue could easily take her place in Richard Daley's Civic Center next to the Picasso "thing" (or, as we call it in Chicago, "da ting").

The figurines are between twelve and twenty thousand years old, and more recently, some have been found in Russia that may be as much as fifty thousand years old. They have ranged from the Pyrenees to Siberia and throughout the Near East and the Orient. Neumann points out that of the sixty Stone Age sculptures available to us at the time of his writing, there were fifty-five female figures and only five male figures. Furthermore, the male figures were poorly executed and did not seem to have any cultic significance. The female figures clearly run to a type and were executed with not inconsiderable skill. While it is not certain that these figures had cultic significance, I think it is apparent that they represent the importance to our cave-dwelling ancestors of those powers in the universe which are perceived to be feminine. For the purposes of this book, such a conclusion seems sufficient.

The figurines do not look very human. The heads are usually shrunken and misshapen, the buttocks and the primary and secondary genital areas are greatly exaggerated. Since we know from skeletal remains that that is not the way Stone Age women looked, and since the artists seemed to be reasonably skillful at making figurines appear as they intended, one has to conclude that the statues are symbolic and hence quite possibly religious. One need not go into elaborate theories of the collective unconscious nor speculate about the bizarre sexual tastes of our predecessors (not much different from ours; perhaps they might well have found the *Playboy* centerfolds a bit bizarre). To conclude, these indeed are figures of a female deity, a Great Mother, the pregnant goddess of fertility, a symbol of the reproducing, protecting, and nourishing dimensions of reality. Neumann puts it nicely:

One means by which early man could represent the numinous magnificence and archetypal uniqueness of the Feminine consisted in an expressive "exaggeration" of form, an
accentuation of the elementary character. Here the body feeling plays a decisive role. The individual who created and the
group which worshipped these works were unquestionably
fascinated and attracted by the corporeity, the exuberant
fullness and massive warmth, that emanate from such a figure. (This is the justification for applying the term "sensuous" to such works.) The attraction is identical with an unconscious accentuation of the infantile, and for this accent
the goddess is an adequate image of the elementary character
of containment. [18]

I see no need to fall back on "unconscious accentuation of the
infantile" any more than the "collective unconscious" to explain
the existence of the Venus figures, though I would not completely
exclude the analytic models in either. The women kept the fires
going in the caves, they brought children into the world to keep
the tribe alive, they held the group together while the men went
out on the hunt, they probably bound up the wounds of the injured hunters and took care of sick children. It is not too much of
a romantic exaggeration, I think, to suspect that they consoled,
caressed, and reassured the exhausted and weary food-searchers,
as well as offering them sexual satisfaction if not affection (and
who are we to say that affection was absent in the caves?). Small
wonder that divine powers were thought to operate through
women.

Fertility was the great mystery, and no sophisticated modern
looking at a newborn child in his mother's arms can escape completely a sense of fascination and mystery at the awesome phenomenon of reproduction and continuation. Fertility was to the
primitives, as well as to many sophisticated people since them,
not only sacred but *the* sacred thing, *the* sacrament, *the* revelation; for it sustained the human race in its existence, whatever
happened to its individual members. As civilization developed it
was also responsible for the continuation of the fields and the
flocks on which the emerging villages, towns, and cities depended for their food, clothing, and continuing sustenance. If

ever there was a manifestation of the divine power, it was in the phenomenon of fertility.

A woman, then, as a locus of fertility was an especially sacred thing. As such, she was the object of both reverence and fear. She was both fascinating and terrifying, something to be worshiped, but also something to be the object of taboos. Divine powers were indeed potentially benign, but they also could be terrifying and destructive. One was wise to be wary when dealing with the sacred.

The hunter, the warrior, the vigilant guardian of the flocks was aware as well of the fact that a woman could "unman" him. In a state of sexual arousal he was no longer capable of hunting food, protecting the flocks from marauding predators, or fighting off enemies. He may also have discovered, though this is problematic and speculative, that once sexually aroused, a woman was capable of far more pleasure than he, as well as almost insatiable sexual demands. When the passions of the women of the tribe were fully unleashed (perhaps during the annual orgy) they were quite capable of thoroughly disrupting the fragile social structure of the tribe.[19]

It seems reasonable to assume that there was both fear of female sexuality as well as awe and reverence for it among primitive and archaic peoples. It was a sacred force, and sacred forces were to be both reverenced and feared. To what extent this fear is responsible for the repression of women in many cultures up to and including the modern is problematic. Many of the customs and social structures which have emerged could as easily be explained by the fact that when infant mortality rates were high (as they have been at all times in human history until very recently), the time and energies of woman were consumed by childbearing and childrearing. Under such circumstances, the secondary role of women in the tribe or in the village or city may have been a custom based more on pragmatic than on protoideological reasons. Still, fear for something sacred may also have played a role. Surely no one even today would say that fear of the opposite sex has completely vanished from the human condition.

Whatever may have been the case in the caves and in the very primitive food-gathering and hunting societies that developed after the Ice Age, it is surely true that by the time we get to the pastoral and agricultural societies at the dawn of history, fertility had become the central theme of religious activity. It was not merely that fertility cults were part of religion; religion had become a fertility cult, for fertility was now the dominant force in human life. The flocks must produce, the fields must spring into life or large numbers of people would starve. When dealing with a force that crucial and that powerful, one simply had to treat it as sacred.

As time passed the goddesses became more human in their appearance and more attractive. By five thousand years ago, Egyptian and Cretan goddesses were quite lovely, and had they appeared on a street in a modern city would doubtless attract more than cursory attention. In addition, certain definite themes were beginning to appear. There is a "madonna" figure from Cyprus which may date from the twentieth century B.C. (Plate 32), and other "madonna" figures discovered in Hittite and Egyptian cultures; indeed Neumann pictures (Plate 38) an Isis with Horus figure from 1700–2000 years B.C. that might almost have come out of the Renaissance. The pietà aspect of goddesses may be found in some pre-Roman Sardinian statues (Plates 46, 47), and extremely nude goddesses from Babylon, Greece, and Crete (Plates 54–56) demonstrate the sexual potency of the female goddess images. (Some of these erotic goddesses, incidentally, are equipped with snakes, suggesting, perhaps, the risk a man runs when he permits himself to be seduced into the body of a woman.)

There are also goddesses of death. Among them is the lovely Egyptian, Nut (a lady one would not mind encountering in life or death (Plates 90, 91); and among those far more fearsome goddesses, whom one would avoid under all circumstances if possible, is the Indian goddess, Kali, the Devourer (Plates 65–67). The ambivalence about the death dimension of the female deity is clear from the art. Kali, for example, is in some of her manifestations truly a fearsome devourer; at other times she is far more gentle and attractive, tender and consoling (Plate 182). In the latter form she seems to be mother or elder sister to the liveliest of all the Eastern goddesses, Tara (Plates 183–185). Similarly Lilith, the Sumerian goddess of death, has strange webbed, clawed feet, but the rest of her is quite nicely feminine (Plate 126).

As prehistory turned into recorded history, the feminine sacred principle began to undergo differentiation. The divine female power was seen as life-giving and life-taking-away. It is from Mother Earth we are born and to Mother Earth we will return in death; it is a woman who brings us into the world and, quite probably, it is a woman who holds in her arms the head of the wounded hunter or warrior or sick child. The Earth Mother who receives us at death could be thought of as either gentle consoler or fierce devourer. Woman further provided sexual mystery and sexual reward. She brought life, pleasure, excitement, death; and the various woman goddesses reflected the implicit conviction that life, pleasure, excitement, and death themselves reflected components of the perfect unity of the ultimate and the absolute.[20]

Joseph Campbell writes about the *Shakti* of Hindu religion and summarizes the symbolism of the female deity (describing the statue of the Javanese Queen Dedes, Shakti of Adi Buddha):

> The important sanskrit term *shakti*, meaning power, capacity, energy, faculty or capability has here been used in a technical sense basic to all Oriental religious thinking, namely to denote the energy or active power of a male divinity as embodied in his spouse. Carried further (by analogy), every wife is her husband's shakti and every beloved woman her lover's. Beatrice was Dante's. Carried further still: the word connotes female spiritual power in general as a manifest; for instance, in the radiance of beauty or on the elemental level in the sheer power of the female sex to work effects on the male. It is operative in the power of the womb to transform seed into fruit, to enclose, protect, and give birth. Analogously on the psychological plane, it is the power of a woman to bring a man to his senses, to let him see himself in a mirror, to lure him to his realization—or destruction.[21]

I would add quickly that the feminine spiritual power is part of the human condition and exists in both men and women. It is called "feminine" because of the obvious analogy between this psychological power (which is present and admirable in both men and women) and the biological functions of the woman. Doubtless this analogy has been widely abused in oppressive distortions of the "eternal feminine" as applied only to women, but such abuse does not invalidate the universal symbolic use of the analogy in virtually all the religions of humankind. Extreme feminist ideologists may not want to use it—and that is their privilege—but they are dissenting from the universal practice of humankind, and in all likelihood from the propensities of the human preconscious (bracketing, as irrelevant to our purposes here, the Jungian paradigm of the collective unconscious).

It is interesting to note—and Campbell does not do it—that some students of ancient Semitic religion think that the "She-kenah" (the "power" or "glory" of Yahweh) was once a female consort of that fierce old desert warrior god long before the Sinai experience of the wandering Hebrews.

To some extent this differentiation of the goddesses into separate categories is artificial. An individual goddess took on many shapes and forms in the different cults that were offered to her. Still, by the time of classical antiquity, there was a rough division of labor established among the goddesses: Venus was not into the same thing that Diana was into, and Athena and Juno tended to have different spheres of action. The experience of sexual differentiation obtained in the encounter with the feminine is, of course, a single experience, but there are many components to it; and those components, from early history to classical antiquity, are more and more sharply discriminated. The giver of life, the sexual lover, the source of inspiration, the receiver in death (either compassionate or destructive)—these are the various ways men encountered women and women came to know themselves in their encounter with men. It was naturally assumed (though implicitly and mythologically rather than metaphysically) that these same characteristics could also be encountered in the absolute and the ultimate. The goddesses acted as intermediaries between the experience of the feminine in ordinary life and the assumed existence of the feminine as a component of the ultimate.

We wonder about the mentality of the artist of these female images. Was he working from mythological insight? To what extent was he simply bemused by the woman who was his model (in his imagination if not in physical presence)? The more ancient the figure the more abstract and mythological seems to have been the artist's perspective. The cave figurines could scarcely have been fascinating as women to the person who carved them; but certainly the more recent (5,000 years ago) Middle Eastern figurines begin to take on enough human characteristics that one suspects the artist was depicting a real woman as well as a divine force. Isis and Nut are goddesses, but they are indeed attractive women, and by the time we get to the Grecian Venuses, one simply has statues of beautiful women to whom the name of a goddess has been attached.

We must remember, however, that the Greeks had no trouble at all seeing their statues as religious. We see them more as beautiful women, because the distinction between the religious and the secular was not nearly as sharp for them as it is for us. If there is a feminine component of the deity, one might argue, there is no reason why that component is any better revealed to us in a Venus of Lespugue than it is in the Venus de Milo. All things are potentially sacraments, and if sexual differentiation is a limit-experience par excellence, there is no reason in the world why the Venus de Milo cannot be a symbol as well as a thing.

And she sure is pretty.

Neumann develops an elaborate paradigm based on Jungian theory to organize humankind's experience of the feminine and the goddesses which symbolize this experience.[22] He sees the experience of the feminine as being ordered along two dimensions, the elementary and the transformation. The elementary, or "central symbolism of the Feminine," is expressed in a generalized equation which purports to schematize the basic experience of the Feminine: Woman = Body = Vessel = World. The central symbolism of the feminine, then, is not the sun so much as the moon. Woman as world or as earth gives life and then takes it back; Woman as moon, as transformer, gives renewal, rebirth. Hence, the two dimensions of the experience of the feminine are the dimension of birth and the dimension of rebirth. Combining these two dimensions, Neumann produces his elaborate paradigm. (See Neumann, p. 82).

The axis "M," running from upper left to lower right of the

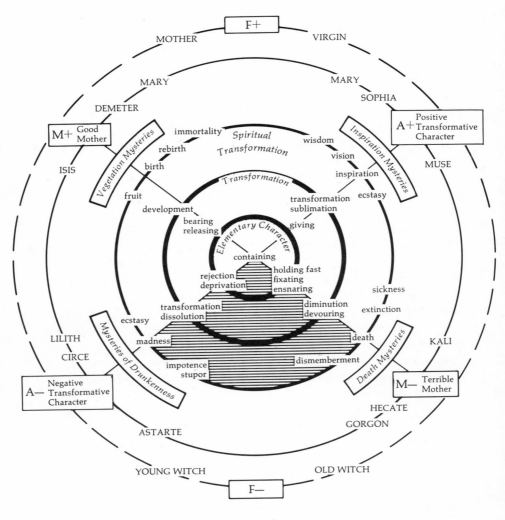

Figure I

circles represents the maternal dimension of the feminine, the woman as the source of the earth and of life, woman as earth from which life springs and as earth to which life returns. The "A" dimension, running from lower left to upper right represents woman as the source of rebirth as transformation, as the moon which seduces and inspires. Both dimensions have a positive and negative pole: a good mother which gives life and a bad mother which destroys it; a positive transformation which exalts the spiritual side of man and a negative transformation which drags him down into ecstasy and pleasure. One has four different kinds of goddesses then: Demeter and Isis, goddesses of fertility; Kali and Gorgon, goddesses of death; the platonic Sophia, the Greek Muse, the Christian Mary (in Neumann's model) as a source of positive spiritual ecstacy, and Astarte (and I might add Venus) as the symbols of physical ecstacy.[23]

So in Neumann's ordering of the data of the history of religions, I observe four different aspects of woman as perceived by both men and women: (1) woman as source of life, (2) woman as inspiration, (3) woman as source of sexual satisfaction, and (4) woman as absorbing in ego-destroying death.

Now of course life, death, inspiration, and pleasure are what human existence is all about; and somehow or other it can be found in every major religious symbol. Religious language does not try to say different things in its various symbols; rather it tries to say the same thing in a different way. Any good religious symbol tries to reveal to us that the ultimate is both the beginning and the end and the occasion of all our inspiration and pleasure. One could rearrange the manifestations of almost any major symbolic theme in a paradigm such as Neumann's. However, because human sexuality is such a powerful and compelling force in our daily life, sexual gods and goddesses reveal to us their "hints of an explanation" with immense force and clarity. They tell us about certain fundamental parameters of human existence and certain fundamental dimensions and structures of the human personality. Some variations on the sexual symbols are more illuminating than others, and none of them, of course, are completely free from the cultural limitations of their own time and place. One turns to the history of religions for symbolic themes, not to seek for perfectly developed symbols but to strive to learn what one can about the propensities of humankind to interpret the varieties of their experience so that, having ordered that experience, they can respond to it.

Neumann's chart is a model, a paradigm, and not a photograph of reality. We human beings do not go around with our brains and memories divided into compartments like those on his chart. Neumann's paradigm, like all good paradigms, is a tentative working model, an ordering of the data which indeed is thought to have some connection with reality but by no means to be a definitive description of it.

In other words, if you find another model more useful for ordering the data of the history of religion and for linking the gods and goddesses with psychological and social experiences of human life, by all means use it. But I think it not unreasonable to suggest that in the experience of the opposite sex (and the traits of the opposite sex one perceives in one's own sexuality) the Other is perceived as linked to the rediscovery of self, the loss of self, pleasure, and inspiration. Neumann's model is a useful way of depicting those experiences.

One can certainly agree that Neumann's schema is a useful way of ordering the data without having to buy the philosophical and psychoanalytic theory that underlies it. Woman as symbol can reveal the universe as giving life or taking it away (either destructively or compassionately); she can also, as symbol, restructure our perceptions to view the universe as inspiring us to nobility of thought and effort, or as seducing us to ecstatic frenzy. This may be a useful way of describing the experience of sexual differentiation as a limit-experience, as one that shatters our old structures of perception and reorders them into new and potentially transforming configurations. Other ways of ordering both the data of our experience and the data from the histories of religion are surely possible. Neumann's seems useful, and I propose to use it with some modifications throughout this book.

What I am about is by now probably clear to the reader. In the next chapter I shall explore the origins of the Mary myth. I will show that even in its beginnings the myth contained, however inchoately, the four themes schematized by Neumann: woman as mother and as death, and woman as source of spiritual inspiration and physical ecstasy. I shall then in subsequent chapters analyze the four experiences of sexual differentiation and Mary's role as a symbol that illumines the ambiguities of these experiences and reveals the feminine aspect of the deity, or, if one wishes to be Heideggerian, reveals the feminine aspect of Being at work in these experiences. If it be true that Mary as Madonna, Virgo, Sponsa, and Pietà can illumine the experiences of sexual differentiation, even in our own time, and by so doing provide us with the new direction that comes from shattering old structures of perceptions in response to our existential needs, then Mary is alive and well and smiling at us just as she did at Henry Adams at Chartres.

As David Tracy has pointed out to me, there are two aspects of sexual differentiation as limit-experience—or perhaps two different though related experiences. In the first, one experiences the gifted-ness, the wonder of sexual differentiation: there is another who is like me yet different, one who is a compliment to me, a challenge to me, a fulfillment of me both biologically and psychologically. I will find (or can find or could find) fullness and completion through union with the other, and that union will not only be serviceable for the species (if I think of that at all) but joyous and "wonder-full" for me.

In the second experience, flowing sometimes but not always from the first, I discover simultaneously the androgyny of the other and the androgyny of myself. There is a rhythm in all intimacies and in heterosexual intimacy particularly. Indeed, the most exciting joy and pleasure frequently come precisely from the rhythmic alternation of roles and functions. One gives then gets; one takes then yields; one conquers then surrenders; one pursues then is pursued; one hides then reveals; one attacks then retreats; one is passive then dominant. In such a rhythm one discovers in the spouse the twin poles of androgyny. The most dainty and shy woman becomes the passionate and aggressive attacker. The most direct and forceful man becomes a weak and passive plaything. There is joy in both the changing roles of the other and of the self. Not only is the spouse capable of playing both masculine and feminine roles, the self is capable of being both masculine and feminine, of releasing with pure delight those aspects of the personality which normally the cultural environment compels him or her to hide.

Sexual intimacy between two humans does not always follow

such rhythm. It is easier to settle into one or the other role and not run the risk of departing from it. But if there are fewer risks, there is also less excitement, less challenge, and less pleasure. A monophonic relationship is not nearly so much fun as a stereophonic one (if I may be excused the metaphor); nor is it so nearly likely to produce either the limit-experience of sexual differentiation or the even more intense limit-experience of discovering the grace and the gracefulness of one's own androgynous personality. In this latter experience one receives a hint—a "rumor" from one of Professor Peter Berger's angels—that the self is most like the ultimate precisely when it is caught up in the rhythm of alternating "masculinity" and "femininity." Surely at the height of passion the rigid role constraints that the culture imposes tend to slip away (although we can resist the tendency), and we experience not merely pleasure but a liberation, a freedom, an abandonment which enables us to be something more than we usually are. As the various components of our personality blend together in an ever more rapid alternation of the masculine and the feminine, of the pursuer and the pursued, we get a hint of what it must be like to be God—the One in whom the pursuer and the pursued (the first and the final cause) are perfectly blended.

There are two errors which must be avoided if one is to understand the symbol as an occasion of a limit-experience and the medium by which that experience is shared with others. First of all, the modernists, who lacked our sophistication in understanding the nature of symbols, as well as the detailed research of such scholars as Eliade, were wrong when they saw the symbol as a kind of free-floating inkblot which could be interpreted by a new age in response to its own problems without any particular respect for the form and structure of the symbol itself. The symbol has its own morphology that cannot be violated by the interpreter precisely because there is built into the thing-which-becomes-symbol a structure and being of its own. The annual rebirth of nature at springtime is a rebirth. One may make many different things of it, but one violates the morphology of the symbol when one claims to see in it, for example, a call for political revolution. Revolution may be appropriate under some circumstances, but it is not the reality revealed by the spring symbol. Spring is not a sacrament of revolution; it is a sacrament of rebirth.

However, while the morphology of the thing-become-symbol gives a certain direction and strain to the limit-experience, which the thing occasions as it becomes symbol, it does not predetermine the nature of the experience, the substance of that which is revealed in the experience, or the content of the limit-language which is later used to describe the experience. The tree indeed calls to mind the fact that heaven and earth are linked, for example, but in Jean Paul Sartre's experience of it, the link was absurd and irrational, while in Avery Dulles's experience the link was gracious and benign. Thus, as wrong as the modernists are those proponents of a "perennial religion" who see all the symbols of the great world religions revealing the same fundamental truths. Rebirth has a very different substantive meaning for those who experienced the first Christian Easter and for those who reexperience it today than it had for their pre-Canaanite ancestors when they celebrated the spring fertility rituals. Easter also went beyond what the first Christians had experienced in their pre-Easter/Passover celebrations.

There was and is morphological similarity (which makes the history of religions possible as an academic discipline) among early nature fertility rites, the Jewish Passover, and the Christian Easter. But there were differences in the content of the experiences and differences in the substance of what is reported through the symbols which re-present those experiences to the faithful. Quite simply, the message of personal survival (of Jesus and eventually of ourselves) that is at the depth of the Easter experience was not present in the nature fertility rituals, and at best only ambiguously present in the Second Temple Jewish Passover. There were hints of such possibilities, but they were not taken seriously or fully. In the Christian Easter, the hint of personal survival becomes the core of the experience and hence the experience itself (both in its original and its re-presented form). It is categorically different from (though not completely unrelated to) its predecessors.

So, too, with the experience of sexual differentiation and the androgyny of God. There are morphological similarities between Mary and the mother goddesses of antiquity; she is not completely unrelated to them. She and they are rooted in the experience of sexual differentiation, as a sacrament of the androgyny, the *coincidentia oppositorum* of the ultimate. But it is rather different feminine aspects of the ultimate which is revealed by Mary than those which are revealed by Kali or even by Tara. The Christian experience of sexual differentiation as sacrament is different from the Indian or Tibetan related experience. The combination of morphological similarity but substantive differences in limit-experience is possible because humans come to such experiences with different existential needs and different antecedent worldviews, and because the symbols are dense, multilayered, polyvalent in their own reality. They are not formless inkblots, but neither are they propositions which admit only of very narrow and restricted interpretation.

It might well be argued that the fertility rites prepared the way for Easter, that Nut (the tender Egyptian goddess of the underworld) prepared the way for Mary. Humankind had to know the paschal lamb of the pre-Sinai Semitic tribes and the Passover of Pharasaic Judaism before it could know the risen Jesus of Easter. It had to know the tender Nut and the life-giving Demeter before it could know Mary the virgin mother.

At one level of argumentation this need hardly be questioned. Human religious consciousness does indeed evolve. But at a deeper level I do not think that we have yet thought through clearly the theological and psychological explanations of the mechanisms by which this progress occurs. Such questions are beyond the scope of the present book.[24] I will be content to assert here that Christian religious experience and Christian religious faith, which is both revealed and re-presented in such experience, is not totally unrelated to humankind's other religious experiences, but it is categorically different from them. I say this not merely because I am a Christian but because the most elementary analysis of what the symbols portray as the core of the Christian experience demonstrates that the Christian experience is drastically different from its antecedents and rivals. Mary may be "like" Tara or Nut or even Kali. It may help us to understand Mary better if we compare her with Tara, Nut, and Kali. We see how she, like they, resulted from the limit-experience of sexual differentiation and reveals an androgynous deity. But unless we are totally blind, we cannot avoid the immediate recognition that Mary is a very different woman than they and reveals a very different kind of deity. It is not merely that Mary is an historical person and that they are not (although that difference is critical); Mary is the only feminine religious symbol who reveals a God passionately in love with his people. You can fear, respect, and even worship Kali and Tara and Nut; but for Mary you write a poem or a love song.

And that is a difference of absolutely decisive importance for the whole of humankind and for the rest of human history.

Some Christians have been uneasy on occasion with the comparison of Mary with her predecessors, sisters, and rivals. They are men and women of faint heart. In any such contest Mary is a sure winner.

Mary, indeed, is part of the tradition of feminine deities, for like her predecessors she reveals the feminine dimension of an androgynous God.[25] But if she is part of this tradition, Mary is clearly superior to it. One need only compare the art inspired by Mary with that inspired by her predecessors to see both the similarities and the striking differences between them. I wonder how students of comparative religion, and those early Catholic apologists who frantically tried to respond to them, could have thought that the similarities eliminated the important differences. I also wonder why the theologians who wrote about Mary in the 1950s and 1960s failed to realize that the history of religion was on their side. One need only compare the images of Kali or of Diana of the Ephesians with, let us say, the young woman in an Annunciation painting by Fra Angelico or Bonfigli to see that one is in very different worlds. It is not of Kali that we sing.

> I sing of a maiden that
> Matchless is,
> King of all Kings is her son
> I wis.
>
> He came all so still
> Where his mother was

As dew in April
   That falleth on grass.

He came all so still
   To his mother's bower
As dew in April
   That falleth on shower.

He came all so still
   Where his mother lay
As dew in April
   That falleth on spray.

Mother and maiden
   Was ne'er none but she
Well may such a lady
   God's mother be.

          "I Sing of a Maiden"—Anonymous

Chapter 4

THE EMERGENCE
OF MARY

There is much that is noble in the pagan goddesses. Fertility, ecstasy, inspiration, reunion with the cosmos in death—all of these qualities could stir up artistic and religious genius. They could also, unfortunately, easily be perverted. Orgies, human sacrifice, ritual prostitution were the dark side of the fertility cults, a dark side which all too often became dominant.

It would be wrong, however, to think that there was no anticipation in the pagan worship of the Queen of Heaven to the Christianization of that cult in the honoring of Mary. On the contrary, despite the sexual excesses and the persistence of human sacrifices beyond boundaries of the empire, there were strains in the pagan cult of the Queen of Heaven which almost seemed to demand transformation. One can almost go so far as to say that if Mary had not come along, the pagans might have had to invent her. The Roman writer Apuleius (in a translation by Robert Graves) describes his experience of the Queen of Heaven in the Isis cult:

> The apparition of a woman began to rise from the middle of the sea with so lovely a face that the gods themselves would have fallen down in adoration of it. First the head, then the whole shining body gradually emerged and stood before me poised on the surface of the waves. . . .
>
> Her long hair fell in tapering ringlets on her lovely neck, and was crowned with an intricate chaplet in which was

73

woven every kind of flower. Just above her brow shone a round disc, like a mirror, or like the bright face of the moon, which told me who she was. Vipers rising from the left-hand and right-hand partings of her hair supported this disc, with ears of corn bristling beside them. Her many-coloured robe was of finest linen; part was glistening white, part crocus-yellow, part glowing red, and along the entire hem a woven bordure of flowers and fruit clung swaying in the breeze. But what caught and held my eye more than anything else was the deep black lustre of her mantle. She wore it slung across her body from the right hip to the left shoulder, where it was caught in a knot resembling the boss of a shield; but part of it hung in innumerable folds, the tasselled fringe quivering. It was embroidered with glittering stars on the hem and everywhere else, and in the middle beamed a full and fiery moon. . . .

All the perfumes of Arabia floated into my nostrils as the Goddess deigned to address me: 'You see me here, Lucius, in answer to your prayer. I am Nature, the universal Mother, mistress of all the elements, primordial child of time, sovereign of all things spiritual, queen of the dead, queen also of the immortals, the single manifestation of all gods and goddesses that are. . . . Though I am worshipped in many aspects, known by countless names, and propitiated with all manner of different rites, yet the whole round earth venerates me.

> [From Apuleius, *The Golden Ass*, Robert Graves' translation, p. 268–71. Robert Graves, *The Greek Myths*, Penguin, 1960.]

Still, there is no point in attempting to gloss over the excesses of the fertility cults, particularly those which were practiced in the land of Canaan by the neighbors of the Hebrews. The things that went on in the high places may not have been as bad as the prophets thought, but they clearly were considerably less than attractive. The consoling and homey aspects of the worship of the Queen of Heaven existed side by side with much more savage practices that to the prophets of official Yahwism were thoroughly unacceptable. We probably need more research to know how depraved the canaanite fertility cults got. But the opposition of the prophets was only in part practical. They could not accept the identification of the deity with the life forces of the cosmos on theoretical grounds even if there were no practical abuses in such cults. The prophetic objection to the fertility cults was finally theological.

Therefore, when Yahweh, that pushy old desert Semitic storm god, elbowed his way into human history in the Sinai experience, he quite pointedly warned his followers against the fertility cult. There was only one god, and his name was Yahweh. Whatever other deities might have existed were inferior to him and not to be taken seriously. The cosmos was his show. As he ironically informed Job, humans were not around when he made it. He was not about to abide any competition from the bizarre deities who had set themselves up in the deity business—either male or female.

Fertility was not excluded from the new Israelite cult, for they, like all other people, needed to insure that the crops would produce food for the coming year. But one did not now guarantee fertility of the fields by worshiping the fertility forces of the universe or by engaging in ritualized sex. One guaranteed fertility by worshiping Yahweh. It was not so much, as Walter Harrelson points out in his brilliant book, *From Fertility Cult to Worship*,[1] that conflict between Yahweh and Baal was one between a god of fertility and a god of history, for Yahweh dominated both history and fertility.

So the old pagan fertility festivals of unleavened bread and the paschal lamb were combined into a new feast which honored not fertility powers but the Lord who dominated fertility and everything else:

> God was the giver of fertility, but Israel could not coerce fertility or even participate in the process through cultic acts. The task of man was radically secularized. Man was to till the soil, remove the rocks, and clear additional acreage. He was to fight the recalcitrant forces of nature in a world twisted by his own sin, wrestling food from the earth. This was his part. The rain came at God's behest; the earth produced because God had arranged in its creation that it should do so. All fruits of the soil, all fruit of the womb, were gifts of God—for Israel as much as for her neighbors.

> What was eliminated was the necessity or even the possi-
> bility for Israel—faithful Israel—to strike some bargain with
> God, to induce the earth to produce or even to participate
> culticly in the earth's renewal.[2]

In fairness to the pagans, who were the neighbors of the Israelites, it must be said that there probably was some kind of
vague distinction in their minds between the powers of fertility
and the god and goddess who animated these powers. But in
popular practice, belief, and cult, this distinction was pretty well
erased. One worshiped the process itself, one integrated one's
life through cultic behavior into the process. One became part of
the divine power of fertility. The symbol, for all practical purposes, had become more than a sacrament and almost the reality
which it revealed. By uniting oneself ritualistically with the symbol, one obtained a certain power over the reality which worked
in and through the symbol. More simply, if one committed ritual
prostitution with a priestess of the fertility goddess, one obtained some kind of power over that goddess (in addition to
whatever personal pleasure one might have experienced) and
constrained the goddess to see that the fertility process would
indeed produce the abundance that the tribe or village needed.

No one constrained Yahweh to do anything. He did what he
did out of his generosity, his goodness, his love. He was not
caught up in these processes of nature; he could not be dealt with
by those who integrated themselves into the process culticly. He
was Yahweh; he did things his way, and nobody forced his hand
with ritual.

The feminine deities, therefore, vanished from the scene. Neumann's suggestion that the "Shekinah," the so-called "glory of
God in exile," is a feminine component of Yahwistic religion is
not very persuasive. There may have been a Shekinah goddess at
some stage of the game, but by the time we come to the Yahwism
of the prophets, she had long since vanished from the scene.

The purified and secularized fertility cult of the Passover, and
the worship of Yahweh as the Lord of history and the Lord of fertility (and Lord of everything else, for that matter) did not, of
course, exorcise the fertility goddesses from the popular religion

of ordinary people. The prophets railed against Baal and his consorts; they warned the Israelites of false worship in "the high places" and against the adoration of idols, most of which were probably fertility gods and goddesses. Yahweh continually warns through his prophetic spokesmen that his people were not to go off "whoring" with false gods. Such a choice of verb leaves little doubt that it was a regression to fertility cultism that they had in mind.

The struggle between Yahwism and the more ancient pagan fertility rituals was a long and fierce one, and while Yahweh had pretty well swept the field clear by the time of the Second Temple, the periodic construction of pagan temples and the willingness of some Jews to worship in them despite the denunciations of both the Pharisees and the temple priesthood indicates that the goddesses may have retreated and gone underground, but they were not completely destroyed.

However, sexual differentiation had by no means been eliminated from the Yahwistic religion. It reappeared in a new and extremely important manifestation. Yehweh was the spouse, Israel was the people, his bride. Yahweh's intervention on Sinai was the beginning of a divine love affair with a fickle, unreliable but still very attractive spouse. Otherwise, why would Yahweh be interested in the first place? This image of the people as the bride of Yahweh caught up in intimate union with a passionate God (the word "passionate" is unfortunately translated as "jealous" in most versions of Exodus 20) is implied even in the very ancient Sinai stories. It becomes obvious and explicit in the sexual imagery of such prophets as Osee, Ezekiel, and Jeremiah. The Christian notion of the church as the spouse of Jesus is obviously indebted to the Jewish symbolism of Yahweh's romance with his people. In the later prophets this romance was frequently symbolized in the figure of the Daughter of Zion. In the rhetoric of Jewish religious writing, there is a technique called "the corporate personality." A single person, real or imaginary, is equated with the whole people. The Daughter of Zion is spoken of frequently as though she were an individual, but in fact she represents the corporate body of Israel. It is the romance between Yahweh and the Daughter of Zion which leads to the conception

and birth of the messianic age. Passages with this theme abound
in the later prophets:

> This Yahweh proclaims to the ends of the earth:
> Say to the daughter of Zion, "Look, your saviour comes,
> the prize of his victory with him, his trophies before him."
>
> (Is 62:11)

> Shout for joy, daughter of Zion,
> Israel, shout aloud!
> Rejoice, exult with all your heart,
> daughter of Jerusalem!
> Yahweh has repealed your sentence;
> he has driven your enemies away.
> Yahweh, the king of Israel, is in your midst;
> you have no more evil to fear.
>
> When that day comes, word will come to Jerusalem:
> Zion, have no fear,
> do not let your hands fall limp.
> Yahweh your God is in your midst,
> a victorious warrior.
> He will exult with joy over you,
> he will renew you by his love;
> he will dance with shouts of joy for you
> as on a day of festival.
>
> (Zp 3:14–18)

> Sing, rejoice,
> daughter of Zion;
> for I am coming
> to dwell in the middle of you
> —it is Yahweh who speaks.
>
> (Zc 2:10 [3])

One can also find liturgical texts which echo the theme:

> In his winepress the Lord has trampled
> the virgin daughter of Judah.   (Lm 1:15)

> How can I describe you, to what compare you,
> daughter of Jerusalem?

Who can rescue and comfort you,
virgin daughter of Zion?   (Lm 2:13)

She has done a deed of horror,
the Virgin of Israel.   (Jr 18:13)

Yes, I hear screams like those of a woman in labour,
anguish like that of a woman giving birth to her first child;
they are the screams of the daughter of Zion, gasping,
hands outstretched.   (Jr 4:31)

Writhe, cry out, daughter of Zion,
like a woman in labour,
for now you have to leave the city
and live in the open country.   (Mi 4:10)

According to such writers as Wilfred Knox and Geoffrey Ashe, the figure of "Wisdom" in the Old Testament is feminine. Knox, in his St. Paul and the Church of the Gentiles (Cambridge 1939) says bluntly that there can be little doubt that personified wisdom is both feminine and "on the divine side of the gulf which separates man from God." She is, he argues, a Hebraeicized version of the Syrian goddess Astarte. In his book The Virgin (London: Routledge and Kegan Paul 1976), Ashe notes that the Jewish community in Elephantiné in Egypt reverenced the Virgin Anath (A canaanite goddess) as in "some sense attached to Yahweh" (p. 31). Anath had many of the wisdom characteristics of Greek Athene. Ashe concludes that "the background presence of a female deity in Judaism toward the beginning of the Christian era is rather more than conjectural. While one set of texts evoked the Virgin Daughter of Zion, another evoked the Virgin Wisdom dwelling in Zion, trailing phantasms of a pagan past behind her" (p. 31).

There were, then, still traces of the female deity even in the most refined manifestation of Yahwism—and much stronger traces, it would appear, in Hebrew folk religion. It is precisely to those traces that we must look if we are to begin to understand the emergence of Mary.

Robert Graves, in his translation of the Song of Songs (London: Collins, 1973), suggests that it was in fact a bridal sword dance performed in honor of Anath, who at that era of her development was a goddess of war and battle (a devourer as well as a virgin?). One need not accept all of Graves' speculations, some of which seem pretty thin, to realize that there was far more myth in the Hebrew religion than one would perceive merely from reading the prophets. Indeed the apocalyptic revival of the post-exilic years probably was a return to the imagery (always modified by the Hebrew sense of history) of Near Eastern creation myths. Yahwism, in other words, was a multifaceted and polyvalent religion with room for many different components, including many survivals from paganism which it had absorbed. The female deity was still around, now either absorbed in the tenderness of Yahweh or continuing as the Daughter of Zion or the Wisom of Zion or as the shadowy patron of human love and marriage.

Sexual differentiation as limit-experience, then, is by no means foreign to the Jewish religion. On the contrary, in the later prophets it became one of the dominant themes. But the sexuality of later Yahwism is quite different from that of the fertility cults. Yahweh dominates fertility completely; sexuality is his gift to humankind, but it is a gift that reflects and symbolizes his love for his people.

The daughter of Zion theme was taken over by the church, which saw itself as a new Zion. Given the religious atmosphere of the time when Christianity developed out of Pharisaic Judaism, such a development is not at all surprising. In retrospect, what is astonishing is that all the old goddesses came creeping out of their caves, went through an extraordinary rehabilitation, and emerged in the person of Mary, the mother of Jesus.

The early Christians were no better disposed than their rabbinic Jewish brothers and cousins to pagan deities. They abhorred the grotesque, depraved, and corrupt rites associated with the residual remnants of fertility worship. The reformulation of the old cults in the gnostic wisdom religions was even less acceptable to the early Christians. Under such circumstances one would have expected the Christians, like their rabbinic Jewish relatives to resist with all the power of their command even the slightest concession to the tradition of the female deities; for these deities, in the circumstances in which the Christians encountered them, were frequently quite depraved and always enemy to the Good News. It wasn't merely Diana of the Ephesians who was the natural enemy of St. Paul; in a few short centuries she, Athene, and Aphrodite were gone. But they were replaced from within the Christian religion itself by a new symbol of the feminine component of God, and it was to emerge as the most powerful of all the feminine sacred personalities. It must have been a surprise for everyone.

As one pours over the history books of the early church, it is not really clear how Mary emerged as the new symbol of the feminine component of God. However, it is clear that by the early second century, Christian writers were speaking of her as the new Eve; by the late second or early third century, drawings of her appeared in the catacombs, and by the middle third or early fourth century, direct and explicit devotion to her was well under way.

There seem to have been two factors at work in the emergence of Mary as an object of devotion. First, the early Christians were caught up in a fantastic exuberance that we can barely imagine today (and which, alas, we all too rarely try to imitate). The excitement of the renewing event of the death and resurrection of Jesus had created an extraordinarily powerful liberating experience for many of those who had become followers of Jesus. They were free from old laws, old fears, old constraints, old customs. The world was new; it had been born again, and therefore the early Christian apologists could proclaim that whatever was good, whatever was true, whatever was beautiful, whatever was admirable in the human condition was not only not opposed to Christians but actually already Christian. Art, music, literature, poetry—there was no opposition between these things and the Christian experience. On the contrary, they were already part of such an experience. The dying Roman Empire might be a political threat but nothing could be a cultural threat to these exuberant and self-confident Christians. Whatever was good was Christian. If the good was somehow mixed with the bad, that was no problem; the bad could be swept away and the Christian remain whole and clean. So the various local deities were transformed into saints, and the feminine goddesses were integrated, rehabilitated, and transformed into Mary. Whatever was good in the worship of the goddesses was already Christian and ought to be saved; and whatever was bad could be excised and dismissed as not constituting a very serious threat. Did there seem to be some similarity between Mary and Diana or Juno or Athene or Aphrodite? The early Chistian shrugged his shoulders. So what? Mary was also strikingly different from her predecessors, and no one could seriously believe that her preeminence could be threatened by those pagans. Thus, I suspect, is the way it went. The early Christians were much more casual about the similarities between Mary and the pagan goddesses than were the later reformers or the counterreformers or the early students of comparative religion and the Catholic apologists who tried to argue against them. The early Christians, unlike their successors, knew what Diana was like; they were much more interested in the differences, not similarities, between her and Mary.

In any event, this exuberance for all things good and for all things human probably created a context in which Mary could emerge as a Christian symbol between the end of the first century and the beginning of the fourth. But the mere existence of such a context does not explain why Mary did in fact emerge.

For this explanation we will turn to the theological method that many of the early Christian writers chose to follow; the "argument from type," or "typology." John McKenzie in his *Dictionary of the Bible* defines it as "an exposition which presents the persons, institutions, or events of the Old Testament as 'types' of persons, events, or institutions in the New Testament." [4] Thus figures and events in one section of Scripture are seen as anticipations (though, at least in the more intelligent typology, *not* as literal predictions) of figures and events in another section of Scripture. The early Christians did not invent this technique; it was already in use in the Old Testament. In Isaiah, for example, the restoration of Israel after the exile is described in the terms of Exodus; hence the restoration is in a sense a reenactment of the Exodus. While it is surely the case that some of the typological arguments of the early Christian writers were exaggerated and almost bizarre in their passionate and convoluted development of allegorical similarities, it is still true that typological argument is not all that different from that used by the historians of religion, or even that used by the Jungian psychologists—that there is a certain unity in human religious experiences. Or, as one might put it from the viewpoint of a believer, there are similar themes in the dialogue between God and man, and an early manifestation of theme may anticipate a later manifestation of it, which in its turn may reflect back to an earlier explication of the theme. In the terms of this book, both the "type" and the "antetype" are the same thing-turned-symbol, the same fundamental insight into the nature of the universe that produced similar structures of perceptions and the ordering of similar new configurations.

God creates, God liberates; Adam symbolizes the former, Moses the latter. The creation and liberation of God are manifested once again in Jesus, who in this symbolic and hence very real sense is both the new Adam and the New Moses. He is a symbol that continues the same limit-experience (or a similar limit-experience) which was integrated earlier in the symbols of Adam and Moses.

The early Christians vigorously used the typological argument that Jesus was the new Adam, and especially in their dialogue with their Jewish confreres. St. Paul himself, very early in the game, had begun to reason in this fashion. But if Jesus is the new Adam, the beginning of a new creation, the first partisan of a new humanity, the father of a renewed humankind, who was the new Eve? If there was a new Adam, there had to be a new Eve. Who was the new mother of us all? The jump could not have seemed very great to the one who first made it. Jesus was the new Adam, the father of us all; Mary, his mother, was the new Eve, the mother of Jesus and the mother of all of us. With that jump, Mary emerged as the Christian symbol of the feminine aspect of the deity. The Christian myth was rooted in the limit-experience of sexual differentiation, the Christian transformation of all the goddesses who had gone before—and perhaps the most powerful religious symbol in the Western heritage was born.

But when did it happen? In attempting to answer this question I encountered a paradox, which, as far as I can find, no one else has noticed. The "new" Scripture studies take away from us virtually all historical information about the mother of Jesus. This is a severe blow to the theologians who have blithely assumed that Scripture provided at least some kind of historical information about Mary upon which they could rely for their theological reflections. But if contemporary exegesis has lost the historical Mary, it has enabled us to find the theological Mary much earlier than the theologians might have expected. From the point of view of the theologian of only moderate sophistication in exegesis, "theologizing" really didn't begin until the second century. One could not therefore expect a Marian theology before that time. There was, of course, some kind of theology in the New Testament, but it was not basically theological as much as it was historical (though the modern theologian would quickly add that it was certainly not history the way we mean history). But for the exegete, the New Testament, while containing important historical elements, is made up essentially of theological reflections by the earliest Christians of their experience of the risen Jesus. Hence the exegete has no problem at all in finding the typological theological reflection going on even in the books of the New Testament. The theologian sees Marian dotrine emerging perhaps in the middle of the second century, while careful, responsible, professional exegetes like Raymond Brown, John McHugh, and Lucien Deiss have no difficulty at all in finding Marian theology in the New Testament itself. And an increasing number of Protestant writers, such as Max Thurian, are also prepared to concede (some gracefully, others not) that there is, particularly in St. John and St. Luke, an unquestionable Marian theology. This discovery, of course, knocks into a cocked hat most of the Reformation-Counterreformation arguments over Mary. One may still legitimately dispute the form and shape of the Marian cult; one can no longer deny the presence of explicitly Marian doctrinal themes in the Gospels.

Note the price that has to be paid for this revolution: if one contends—and I believe now that one must—that what the New Testament has to say about Mary is theological, typological, and symbolic reflection for the most part, one has placed Marian themes back almost to the beginning of Chistian reflection. But the cost is the loss of virtually all historically reliable information about Mary herself. In terms of unity among Christians and understanding of Mary as a symbol articulating the limit-experience of sexual differentiation as a revelation of the feminine component of God, the cost may not seem too great; but for those whose devotion to Mary has always depended on the possession of solid historical fact, it may be a devastating blow indeed. We have placed a theological or a symbolic Mary back to almost the beginning of things, but what has happened to the real woman who was the mother at Bethlehem and the mother at the foot of the cross? Do we have the symbolic Madonna and Pietà at the cost of having lost the real one?

We surely have lost precise, detailed information about the historical Madonna and Pietà. We know nothing of what she looked like, what she thought, how she responded to critical situations—at least we know nothing with any kind of historical confidence. The absence of such precise, actual historical knowledge may not be too great a price to pay as long as we do not lose Mary as an actual, historical person. If the Mary symbol becomes detached completely from the actual Mary, then however admirable the symbol may be, it cannot really claim to be Christian. Christianity, like Judaism, is a historical religion. (Though, as my colleague and friend Roland Murphy points out to me repeatedly, it is not merely a historical religion. Salvation history is a basic and fundamental theme of Yahwism; it is not the only theme.)

If Mary is a symbol divorced from a historical personage, then she certainly is an admirable substitute for some of her depraved predecessors, but she is not then a sacrament, a revelatory thing of the God of history who presides over history.

However, I do not think this is a serious problem. We do know that Jesus had a mother. We know that there was a woman who brought him into the world, and we know much about him—his enthusiasm, his passionate sense of urgency, his joyfulness, his sense of intimate union with the Father, his flaming proclamation of the victory of good over evil and of life over death, his promise of resurrection for all of us. We know his courage, his wisdom, his insight, his incredible command of poetic language. We know the startling, shattering, disturbing, paradoxical nature of the language he used in his proverbs, his proclamations, his parables. In knowing him, we surely know much about his mother in the sense that anyone who knows a remarkable man must postulate a remarkable mother. This is not, I would submit, a sentimental romanticism. It is a solid psychological truth. The mother of Jesus had to be an extraordinarily intelligent, courageous, devout, and charming woman. She could hardly have been anything else. It would seem to me that this solid psychological truth provides us with all the historical information we really need—as pleasant as it would be to have more. I think it more than justifies virtually all the devout reflection that believing Christians have traditionally made on the New Testament data. While these data can no longer be considered historically valid, they still may be viewed theologically and are perfectly compatible with the kind of person that Mary must have been. No one can take the mother of God away from us; only a fool would try.

David Tracy, commenting on an earlier version of this manuscript, has noted that it would be a mistake to concede that this mode of knowing Mary through Jesus is a second-class form of knowledge. On the contrary, we know more about the kind of person Mary must have been from the study of her son than we would from the stories in the Scriptures themselves, even if those stories were as historically precise as an account in the morning's *New York Times*. Suppose that you knew a handful of incidents in the life of a woman. Then you met her son and had an opportunity to be with him for a substantial period of time, to listen to his teaching and to observe his actions. Would you think that the few facts about his mother were more important than the certain judgments you would make about her from knowing him? Jesus as the source of our knowledge about his mother is a much better "sacrament" (revelation of truth) than are the New Testament stories about her—whatever historical value these stories may have. Do you know more about Mary from her obedience to the angel or from the knowledge of Jesus her son?

There is profound psychological truth in this concept of the son as sacrament of the mother. But there is also truth in the opposite direction. If we know Mary through Jesus, then having reflected on what his mother must have been like, we come back to Jesus and know him better. The mother is also the sacrament of the son. When we know Mary through Jesus we are able to translate the qualities of Jesus into "feminine" form; and by seeing the feminine sources of the personality of Jesus, we are able to return to that personality and see more easily and readily the feminine aspects of the personality itself. By knowing Mary through Jesus, in other words, we are able to come to terms more fully with the androgyny of the personality of Jesus, and thus we know Jesus through Mary.

And through the two of them there is revealed to us the fullness of the unity of opposites in God. It is by knowing Mary through Jesus and Jesus through Mary that we encounter the androgynous. I hesitate to speak of psychological inevitabilities or necessities in such matters as this, but it is still difficult to see how this perennial human insight of the *coincidentia oppositorum* could have been integrated into the Christian religious tradition—and transformed by it—unless there was some relationship like that between Jesus and Mary. A woman whom Jesus reveals and in whom he is revealed seems to be psychologically indispensable for the Christian religious vision. Indispensable or not, such a woman certainly emerged historically.

I must insist that the comments of the past three paragraphs may be stated in the terminology of contemporary psychology, but they are not merely speculative. They are a description of what in historical fact has been the role of Marian devotion in Catholic Christianity. Catholic devotion to Mary is not based merely or even primarily on the handful of incidents—as beautiful as they may be—related in Scripture. It is based principally on the knowledge of her son. With that knowledge we return to the scriptural incidents and interpret them in light of what we know she must have been because of who her son was. I am not proposing, therefore, any new form of knowledge about Mary but merely pointing out what our knowledge of her has always been and the sound psychological foundations on which that knowledge is based.

I find myself wondering if perhaps we might not be able to say something more—though here I am out on a very long limb. The traditions which the authors of John and Luke have reworked as the basis of their theological reflection are clearly much older than the two Gospels. Apparently they go back to Palestinian sources which may be as old as the middle of the first century. (Indeed it is possible that they may go back to a single common source. There seems to be a relation between the Johannine and Lucan Marian sources, and there is certainly a relationship between their theological reflections.) Whence came these stories? We do not know at present, and it would be a return to the gratuitous confusion of the piety and history which marked an earlier generation of Catholic writing to say that traditions could be traced to Mary herself. But one need not, I think, go that far. If they are not necessarily traditions from Mary, might they not be traditions about Mary as an actual person? It is safe to assume that there were people in the early church who knew her and who were fascinated by her as the mother of Jesus. If her personality was as strong and vigorous as it almost must have been to have been the mother of such a son, it seems reasonable to imagine that she must have had an extraordinary impact on those who knew her. Could it be that the ease with which the church began to theologize about Mary so early, probably even before Luke's Gospel was written, could be explained by the contact that some of the early Christians had with the person herself?

At best, Mary casts but a fleeting shadow across the pages of the New Testament; but it was a very long one indeed, stretching down through the whole history of Christianity.

The principal sources of New Testament theological reflection on Mary as the new Eve are contained in the Lucan infancy stories and in the Johannine Cana-cross narratives. The best available treatment of Luke is contained in John McHugh's *The Mother of Jesus in the New Testament* [5] and the best commentary on the Johannine passages is to be found in Raymond Brown's Anchor commentary. [6]

I shall not endeavor to repeat in detail the brilliant exegetical arguments of these authors. Each should be read in its entirety. However, after reading two commentaries, there can be little reason to question that the typological theme of Mary as Daughter of Zion, the New Eve, the Church, and the Virgin were already strongly at work in the church by the year A.D. 70.

How explicit the Daughter of Zion theme was in the mind of the author of Luke is a matter of minor scholarly debate. Lucien Deiss has no doubt at all that it was in the author's mind explicitly. Max Thurian parallels passages from Luke and from Zephaniah which certainly seem to support the notion that the author was deliberately imitating Zephaniah:

Zeph. 3	*Luke 1*
14. Sing aloud, O daughter of Zion! Shout with delight, O Israel! Rejoice thou, and exult with all your heart, O daughter of Jerusalem!	28. Rejoice thou, full of grace!
15. The Lord has taken away the judgements against you, he has cast out your enemies. The King of Israel, the Lord is in your midst; You shall fear evil no more.	(30. for you have found favour with God.) the Lord is with thee. (33. He will reign over the house of Jacob for ever . . .)
16. On that day it shall be said to Jerusalem: Do not fear, O Zion; let not your hands grow weak. 17. The Lord your God is in your midst,	30. Do not be afraid, Mary; for you have found favour with God. 31. Behold, you will conceive in your womb and bear a son and you will call his name JESUS (Yahweh Saviour).

a victorious Saviour.
He will rejoice over you with
gladness;
he will renew you in his love.
He will exult over you with
loud singing
as on a day of festival.

> The original Hebrew of the Lucan account would make quite
> obvious these literary similarities between the messianic
> proclamation of Zephaniah to the daughter of Zion and the
> angelic Annunciation to Mary, but even the Greek text
> makes it clear.[7]

McHugh implies somewhat more cautiously that the influence
of Zephaniah on Luke may have been preconscious or unconscious: "If anyone had asked him outright, 'Do you mean that
Mary is the Daughter of Zion foretold by the prophets?', he
would have replied that this title summed up perfectly all that he
meant to say."[8]

So Mary, then, either implicitly or explicitly becomes a corporate personality in the infancy stories. She is the spouse of
Yahweh representing the whole people to whom Yahweh is committed in passionate love. Jesus is born of the love between
Israel, as represented by Mary, and Yahweh. Note well that this
is not the pious reflection of a later age. This is the response of
the very early church to a powerful limit-experience. It is proto-
Christian theology, arising out of the awesome shattering of old
structures of perception that was caused by the Christ event.

The Eve-Church typology in which Mary is seen simultaneously as the New Eve and as the Church, the mother of the
new creation, the loving mother of us all, becomes quite explicit
in John's Gospel. Raymond Brown has no problem in seeing the
"woman" in the apocalypse relating to Mary as "woman" in the
Cana narratives, and Mary as "woman" at the foot of the cross.

Two paragraphs in Father Brown's commentary summarize his
careful analysis:

> Having seen the relationship of the three scenes in the
> Johannine corpus in which the woman (Mary, the mother of
> the Messiah, as a symbol of the Church) appears, we may
> now interpret the conversation at Cana. On a theological
> level it can be seen that Mary's request, whether by her in-
> tention or not, would lead to Jesus' performing a sign. Before
> he does perform this sign, Jesus must make clear his refusal
> of Mary's intervention; she cannot have any role in his min-
> istry; his signs must reflect his Father's sovereignty, and not
> any human, or family agency. But if Mary is to have no role

during the ministry, she is to receive a role when *the hour* of his glorification comes, the hour of passion, death, resurrection, and ascension. John thinks of Mary against the background of Gen iii: she is the mother of the Messiah; her role is in the struggle against the satanic serpent, and that struggle comes to its climax in Jesus' hour. Then she will appear at the foot of the cross to be entrusted with offspring whom she must protect in the continuing struggle between Satan and the followers of the Messiah. Mary is the New Eve, the symbol of the Church, the Church has no role during the ministry of Jesus but only after the hour of his resurrection and ascension.[9]

Several years later, in his commentary on John's crucifixion account, Brown repeats, completes, and qualifies ever so slightly the same analysis:

> Jesus' mother is the New Eve who, in imitation of her prototype, the "woman" of Gen ii–iv, can say: "With the help of the Lord I have begotten a man" (cf. Gen iv 1—Feuillet, "Les adieux," pp. 474–77). Perhaps we may also relate Mary the New Eve to Gen iii 15, a passage that describes a struggle between the offspring of Eve and the offspring of the serpent, for "the hour" of Jesus is the hour of the fall of the Prince of this world (John xii 23,31). The symbolism of the Fourth Gospel has a certain resemblance to that of Rev xii 5, 17 where a woman gives birth to the Messiah in the presence of the Satanic dragon or ancient serpent of Genesis, and yet also has other offspring who are the targets of Satan's wrath after the Messiah has been taken to heaven. It is interesting that the offspring of the woman in Revelation are described as "those who keep the commandments of God"; for in John xiv 21–23 we are told that those who keep the commandments are loved by Father and Son, so that a beloved disciple is one who keeps the commandments.
>
> By way of summary, then, we may say that the Johannine picture of Jesus' mother becoming the mother of the Beloved Disciple seems to evoke the OT themes of Lady Zion's giving birth to a new people in the messianic age, and of Eve and her offspring. This imagery flows over into the imagery of the Church who brings forth children modeled after Jesus, and the relationship of loving care that must bind the chil-

dren to their mother. We do not wish to press the details of
this symbolism or to pretend that it is without obscurity. But
there are enough confirmations to give reasonable assurance
that we are on the right track. Such a symbolism makes in-
telligible John's evaluation (xix 28) that this episode at the
foot of the cross is the completion of the work that the Father
has given Jesus to do, in the context of the fulfillment of
Scripture. Certainly the symbolism we have proposed is
scriptural (and thus this episode of the crucifixion falls into
line with the other episodes that emphasize Scripture so
strongly). And since the symbolism is centered on Jesus'
provision for the future of those who believe in him, in
many ways it does complete his work. He shows to the very
end his love for his own (xiii 1), for symbolically he now
provides a communal context of mutual love in which they
shall live after he is gone. The revelatory formula "here is
. . ." on which we have commented, is truly appropriate in
this scene, since Jesus' mother and the Beloved Disciple are
being established in a new relationship representative of
that which will bind the Church and the Christian.[10]

So, in the two Johannine passages of Cana and crucifixion we
see the three symbols combined: the New Eve, the Church, and
the fruitful Daughter Zion. Brown carefully notes that these theological themes in John must be kept distinct from a later Mariology "which will attach importance to the person of Mary herself; . . . the Johannine stress is on Mary as symbol of the
church. Both in Luke and in John, Mariology is incipient and is
expressed in terms of collective personality." [11] A Marian theology, then, is present in incipient form in both Gospels, although
it is a theology of type, of collective personality and not a theology of devotion to an individual person. One may choose to see
in it three symbols or one; either Eve, Church, and Daughter of
Zion, or simply Mother. It is the limit-experience of maternity
that produces the thing-turned-symbol that Mary the mother of
Jesus has become in these two Gospels. In subsequent chapters
of this book, I choose to use the three symbols to fit my four-cell
paradigm, because there are different emphases in each of the
three symbols. The Daughter of Zion is the beloved spouse, the
Sponsa of Yahweh; Eve, the mother of us all, is the Madonna,

and the Church (with perhaps some stretching) is the loving mother who gives us life, and then as Pietà receives us back into death.

There remains the virgin symbolism in Luke's nativity story. It is generally agreed by exegetes that Luke did intend to teach the virginal conception of Jesus. The debate current among exegetes is whether the theological discussion of the virginal conception of Jesus in Matthew and Luke is in fact a theologoumenon, that is, a story created to make a theological point, or whether it is a reflection on historical fact. The two principal Catholic writers who have addressed themselves to this question, Brown and McHugh, differ somewhat. McHugh is far more confident than Brown that the account of the virginal conception is not a theologoumenon. Brown insists that "Scripturally I judge that it is harder to explain the virginal conception by positing theological creation than by positing fact." [12]

I am not qualified to comment on the discussion, although I agree with Brown's point that "it should be clarified for Catholics that the doctrines of the sanctity of Mary and of the incarnation of God's Son are not logically dependent on the virginal conception." [13]

In other words, the power of the Mary symbol remains unshaken no matter how the exegetical discussion is finally resolved. As Brown notes, the fact that all generations have called Mary blessed depends much more on the fact that she was the mother of Jesus than on biological phenomenon or exegetical debate.

I would add that as important as the discussion is and as intelligent and courageous as is the work of such gifted scholars as Father Brown, it would be a mistake for all Catholic attention to be fixed on what is fundamentally a technical issue within the subject of Mary. I have noticed that as I discuss the themes in this book with Catholics such immature (at least it seems so to me) fixation prevents many Catholics from paying attention to Mary's central role as a symbol growing out of the limit-experience of sexual differentiation and revealing the feminine component of God—of being a sacrament of the ultimate as being passionately tender.

But how do we relate the Virgin Mother symbol to the other three New Testament symbols of Mary (as a corporate personality if not as an individual)? Brown says that "Matthew and Luke are interested in virginal conception as a sign of divine choice and grace, and as the idiom of a Christological insight that Jesus was God's Son or the Davidic Messiah from birth . . ." [14] I think more can be said. Virgin Mother is limit-language par excellence. It is disconcerting, shattering, disturbing, and paradoxical, as all good limit-language should be. I would suggest that the purpose of this limit-language is to reveal to us (is to be a sacrament for us) that with the coming of Jesus a new creation began. Just as Adam had no father but God, so Jesus had no father but God. With the coming of Jesus humankind is renewed, decisively and dramatically. The virgin part of the Virgin Mother paradox (a classic example, incidentally, of the tension-intensification dynamism at work in limit-language) emphasizes the total renewal of the human condition that took place in the coming of Jesus, which is precisely what Neumann's Jungian model says is the function of the "positive transformative" character of the feminine archetype. Mary the Virgin, it will be remembered, represents transformation, sublimation, renewal, a new beginning on Neumann's schema.

So all four of the New Testament Marian symbols, Daughter of Zion (Sponsa), Eve (Madonna), Church (Pietà), and Virgin Mother (Virgo), are related to the central theme that with the coming of Jesus humankind began again. Jesus was the new Adam, marking the beginning of a New Creation and the dawn of a new day for humanity. His mother was a new Eve, the bride of Yahweh, the Church who tenderly cares for us after the departure of Jesus. And the virgin-mother represents in her virginity the total renewal of creation.

There were, then, elements of both the Jewish and Christian scriptures that could provide justification for the transformation of the pagan Queen of Heaven—the pagan manifestation of the femininity of God—into a Christian Queen of Heaven. We know very little, however, of the precise history of this transformation. It was certainly linked with the decision of the early church to absorb all that was good, useful, and beautiful in paganism—a decision of great courage and even greater hope. (And we do not know precisely how this decision was made either.) However, once it was determined that, unlike official Jewish Yahweism, official Christian Yahweism had nothing to fear from baptizing pagan customs and cults, the popularity of the Queen of Heaven was such that she surely was going to emerge in Christian dress.

Geoffrey Ashe * has the best available summary of the historical information available to us presently. His thesis of a popular mariology that preceded the official cult (and about which the official church had some doubts at first) is persuasive, although his speculation about a formal underground Marian church that actually worshiped Mary is based on extremely slender grounds, I think.

It also seems reasonable to agree with Ashe—at least until later research proves him wrong—that the turning point was the triumph of popular devotion over official hesitation at the Council of Ephesus. Ashe thinks that the emergence of Mary as *Mother* in the fifth century (in the fourth century she was predominantly *Virgo*) was a response of Christianity to the horrors of pagan invasion by seeking protection and security in the arms of a mother. Ashe's comparison of the religious functions of Mary with those of her predecessor's in enlightening, even though it must be considered speculative because we have no other evidence of what was on the minds of our fifth-century predecessors.**

> The citadel had fallen. Proclus, who had launched the attack, became Patriarch of Constantinople. Rome itself took the lead in a proliferation of Marian churches, new or re-

* Geoffrey Ashe, *The Virgin* (London: Routledge & Kegan Paul, 1976).

** Another useful work with a good deal of information on the scriptural as well as Apocryphal origins of the Mary cult—and some helpful psychological and anthropological speculation—is *Alone of All Her Sex, the Myth and Cult of the Virgin Mary* by Marina Warner (Knopf, 1976). Unfortunately Ms. Warner's work is not free from an ideologically rigid anti-Catholicism. Her concluding prediction ("The virgin will recede into legend . . . emptied of moral significance and [of] . . . its . . . real powers to heal and harm.") is what one would expect from a young woman who believes her own age is the hinge of human history. Ms. Warner's predictions may of course be right, but one may be pardoned for withholding final judgment till more data are in. Mary has been around a long time and is not likely to vanish just because Ms. Warner thinks she has become obsolete.

dedicated. Its own Santa Maria Maggiore quickly acquired a vast mosaic on a triumphal arch, depicting the Virgin enthroned and glorified. Almost every large city throughout the Empire followed suit in architectural homage. Predictably perhaps, several of Mary's churches stood on ground once sacred to female divinity. Santa Maria Maggiore replaced Cybele's temple on the Esquiline hill. In due course Santa Maria in Arocoeli, on the Capitoline, succeeded to a temple of the Phoenician goddess Tanit. Another Roman church adjoined Isis's sanctuary near the Pantheon, another was on a site which had long been consecrated to Minerva, the Roman form of Athene. This last goddess, virgin daughter of Zeus, handed over to the new Virgin in a number of places, notably the Greek city of Syracuse, and Athens itself.

The lingering popular cults made the same transition. Rustic shrines of Aphrodite in Cyprus turned painlessly into shrines of Mary, where she is hailed to this day as *Panaghia Aphroditessa*. Goddesses surrendered their functions to her. Like Cybele she guarded Rome. Like Athene she protected various other cities. Like Isis she watched over seafarers, becoming, and remaining, the 'Star of the Sea'. Like Juno she cared for pregnant women. Christian art reflected Her new attributes. She wore a crown recalling Cybele's. Enthroned with her Child she resembled Isis with Horus. She even had touches of Neith about her. The title and office of Queen of Heaven passed to her naturally from Isis, Anath and Astarte, and preserved her own Collyridian character.

(Ashe, pp. 192–193)

The historical questions of the precise process of the rise of the cult of the Virgin remain to be answered. However, for the purposes of this book, it is enough to say that there seems to be a thrust in human religions to search out symbols that reflect the femininity of God. Such symbols were available—though perhaps vaguely—in the official Yahwism of the Second Temple era and in the surrounding matrix of Graeco-Roman culture. They found their way into the New Testament. After some hesitation, Christians decided that it was safe for them to let these symbols develop into a Christianized cult of the Queen of Heaven. Such a process was practically inevitable once Christianity decided to take the risk of absorbing all that was good and beautiful in paganism.

Prophetic Yahwism—as part of the great "axial era" of human history—discovered a God who ruled supreme over the forces of nature but was independent of them. The prophets objected theologically to the Queen of Heaven cult because they could not reconcile the cult with the transcendent God to which they were committed. Later on, Christian Yahwism would restore the Queen of Heaven to her throne because in the explosion of hope that was the Easter experience, Christians were able to be far more confident of their ability to honor a God who was love without falling into either the excesses of the fertility cults or the theological error of transcendentalized God. This confidence does not seem to have been misplaced. The fear of the prophets was not the fear of reformers. Whatever might be said about the mistakes and excesses that have sometimes marred the Mary cult, the new Queen of Heaven presided over no orgies and affected not in the slightest faith in divine transcendence.

The reformers, incidentally, are not to be blamed for misunderstanding the concern of the prophets; they did not have available the conceptual tools or the research evidence we have.

The question must remain, however, as to whether the paradigm of the female deity as mother, virgin, spouse, and death is a construct of contemporary scholars useful for ordering the data yet fundamentally artificial or whether it reflects a conscious model used by the ancients. Did they see four distinct but overlapping functions of the female deity?

There is evidence to believe that the ancient Celts were quite explicit about the paradigm, and that the pre-Celtic peoples of Ireland also may have consciously distinguished between the (connected) roles of the woman-god. Thus Irish mythology deals with various triads of goddesses responsible for birth, mating (combining the virgo and sponsa roles), and death. The triadic goddesses are variously known as Morrigan, Machu, and Badh; or Danu, Anu, and Brid(get); or Banba, Eriu (whence the name Erin—Ireland), and Aodhla. Their roles overlap and sometimes they change roles, with who does what depending on who is telling the story. Often the high king of Ireland is having ritual intercourse with several of them (busy man, he).

Without going into the complexities of Irish mythology in elaborate detail,* it is clear that the functional distinction of roles was a self-conscious model among the Celts. Furthermore, according to some speculations, the famous triple spiral in the Newgrange Passage tomb (County Meath) also represents the three aspects of the role of the feminine divinity in the continuous pilgrimage of man through life—birth, reproduction, and death (see figure on p. oo). Explicit and self-conscious modeling of the different functions of the earth mother, then, goes back a long, long time—perhaps as much as 5,000 years.**

These are not, I must insist, themes of a later piety, of a medieval personal Mariology or a pious sentiment. These themes are more or less explicit in the New Testament, antedate the writings of the New Testament books, and go back very close to the beginnings of Christianity itself. They are also themes which correspond to the various symbols of the feminine as sacrament, as revelatory of the female component of the godhead, and are also to be found among the goddesses whom Mary replaced.*** The question remains whether these themes might continue to be adequate expressions of the limit-experience of sexual differentiation as we encounter that experience today. Do the themes of Madonna, Sponsa, Virgo, and Pietà still shatter our old structures of perception and reorganize them into new configurations in which we can find light, illumination, and direction for our lives?

> The Christ-child lay on Mary's lap,
> His hair was like a light.

* See, for example, John Sharkey, *Celtic Mysteries* (London: Thames and Huston, 1975).

** For an imaginative modern presentation in the ancient Celtic style of the various Irish goddesses, see Jim Fitzpatrick, *Celtia* (Dublin: De Danann Press, 1975).

*** I am grateful to my friend Herman Schmid, S.J. for pointing out to me that the first Christian Feast of Mary is the feast of "Conceptio Christi"; it was celebrated on a special Sunday of the year probably in the first century—the same Sunday on which the creation of the world and the resurrection were also celebrated. The first Christian feast, really only a special Sunday since all Sundays were resurrection days, then linked creation, conception, and resurrection.

(O weary, weary were the world,
  But here is all aright.)

The Christ-child lay on Mary's breast.
  His hair was like a star.
(O stern and cunning are the kings,
  But here the true hearts are.)

The Christ-child lay on Mary's heart,
  His hair was like a fire.
(O weary, weary is the world,
  But here the world's desire.)

The Christ-child stood at Mary's knee,
  His hair was like a crown,
And all the flowers looked up at Him,
  And all the stars looked down.

G. K. Chesterton, A Christmas Carol

Part II

MADONNA

CELTIC MADONNA

What do you see, freckle-faced mother
Out there at the horizon's line?
Your steel blue eyes miss not a move
And your vise-like mind retains it all.
Friend or foe? You're not yet sure
Probably a friend, so that's okay
But whoever, be fairly warned.
"Touch this kid of mine
And you'll get a bloody nose."

Strong arms, clenched fist, tough jaw
Red-haired Irish beauty indeed
And ready to smile and laugh
And set the whole world dancing
    with her own lilting spirit song
But "mess with this son of mine
    and you'll end on the flat of your back."

"O, it's only you, creation's Lord
Sure, come right on in
Yes, he's a very nice boy
We'll keep him, thank you much,
I'll take care of him for you
Because he's only mine for awhile
But as long as I'm in charge
You won't have to work overtime."

Not a warlike race
Given to peace and love
Never started a fight
But never about to run.

"A fierce woman?
Oh, no, not me
I just take care of my own
Your mother would understand."

The physical foe will be put to rout
And the newer psychic demon exorcised
He'll be free to grow
And accept himself

And chase his dazzling dreams
And never doubt the ground of love
On which we stand and from which he came.
And anyone who messes with him
Will get a bloody nose.

Mystic boy, tow-haired son
    of neighborhood jumprope champ
The world is in your eyes
Your mother has offered it to you
Warm and sensitive you will always be
Life is more painful when intense
But also much better fun
Laugh the way she laughs
Fight the way she fights
Live the way she lives
You may get a few more bloody noses
But also a lot more passionate love.

                          A.M.G.

Chapter **5**

MADONNA
DEI MATER ALMA

Before I turn to my paradigm I want to insist that the exercise in which I am engaged is one of reflection and explication and not of persuasion. When one deals with religious symbols, one does not argue about them. One merely lays out the symbol for people to look at. If they are attracted to it or transformed by it, fine. If not, no amount of argument will persuade them. I am not engaged in any enterprise of trying to sell Marian symbols to anyone. I think the impact of the Enlightenment is so powerful on America's intellectual elite that no symbol, however transforming its character, can possibly speak to them. Things are things, and that's that. If one assumes on *a priori* grounds that there is no graciousness, then surely one will not encounter grace in anything. Heilbroner's hope that Atlas may be a transforming myth is, I think, doomed to be frustrated.

Nor do I wish to persuade my Protestant brothers and sisters that they have been missing something as a result of their fierce exclusion of Mary from the theological and devotional lives. Some Protestants see that already, many do not. I have no ambition to force insight on those who will not receive it.

Finally I am not trying to sell anything to Catholics. The traditional Mariologists—few as these may be—will be far too scandalized by what I have attempted even to listen to me. The more modern, sophisticated Catholics will dismiss my efforts as a frivolous attempt to resuscitate religious symbols which are long-since dead. I have no doubt that some brittle, bitchy, feminist reviewer will tell me that modern liberated woman simply cannot find anything meaningful in Marian symbolism. So be it.

I do not with to argue with modern Catholics, traditional Catholics, Protestants, atheists, Jews, agnostics, women. I am not arguing with anyone. I am describing a symbol system and hinting at some of the implications and illuminations that might exist there for our world. It may be possible that Mary can still ignite grace-revealing limit-experiences for some humans. It is for those who are willing to admit this possibility and for them only that I am writing. Those who want to argue should find someone else to argue with.

I propose to take each one of the four major Marian themes—Madonna, Virgo, Sponsa, Pietà—and run it through a paradigm of fourteen cells. Figure 1 (p. 64) both illustrates the paradigm and applies it to the theme of the present chapter.

First we describe the aspect of sexual differentiation which in the given context has the capacity to produce limit-experience (Experience of Sexual Differentiation). Then we look at the biological roots of this capacity (Biological Origin), and the broad archetypal symbol which expresses this biological reality (Cognate Symbols). We will then consider the pagan goddesses who incarnate the experience (Ancient Goddesses). Next we will see the New Testament origins of the typology which applies this limit-experience to Mary (Type), and then we describe how Christians have described Mary as the thing-turned-symbol (Mary Symbol).

We then examine the existential need which predisposes us for the limit-experience in question (Existential Need); and then we explore the perception-shattering aspect of the limit-experience itself (Limit-Experience). Then we will see what kind of grace is revealed to us in the shattering experience (Grace that is Given), what illumination is obtained and organized into the new configuration of perception (Illumination). Next we turn to the results of the limit-experience which was initiated by the Marian symbol (Action). What are its implications for action in our contemporary world? What does it reveal for a man's self-understanding and a woman for hers (Man-Woman Implication)?

Finally, we give an example of the symbol in poetry (Poem) and art (Plastic Art).

There is a dialectic involved between the overarching symbol and our own symbolic experience which must be kept in mind. We experience maternity as it is disclosed in the world around us; we then encounter Mary as Madonna, perhaps in a leap of imagination from a specific maternity experience of ours. Human-as-mother calls to mind Mary-as-mother, and Mary illumines human-as-mother. The overarching symbol, then, has the power to invervene in a particular limit-experience of ours to bestow sacramental power on the thing we have experienced. There are then really two symbols at work though they may be linked into one symbolism. It is the presence in our life or our cultural background of Mary as Madonna which enables us, or perhaps merely disposes us, to see the grace of the Madonna in an encounter with that aspect of sexual differentiation which we call maternity. The Madonna, in other words, illumines the world in which we live so that the various things we encounter acquire a much stronger potentiality for breaking through the barriers of the hardened structures of our perceptions and engaging in revelatory dialogue with our existential needs.

The most elemental dimension of the experience of sexual differentiation is maternity. Biologically, psychologically, and theologically the image of the mother is primal, and indeed all the other images of woman are derived from it and flow back into it. (Hence the verses of the *Ave Maris Stella* must be rearranged somewhat so that we consider first of all the Madonna theme.)

There are three different ways in which we can experience maternity, each one of which has a powerful potentiality for inducing a limit-experience. Each of us had a mother. It was the primal biological relationship of our lives, and one of the two most important psychological relationships in the development of our personality. We have, of course, internalized our mother; and whether she is alive or dead, her image is permanently implanted in our personality, and we carry it with us for the rest of our lives.

Secondly, many of us have been and are mothers, or are married to women who are mothers. We know not merely what it is like to be brought into the world, nurtured, protected, cared for, played with, admired, loved by a mother; but we also know, either immediately or through observation, what it is like for a woman to bring her own child into the world and to nurture it, protect it, play with it, admire it, love it (and occasionally also to shout at it, discipline it, and wish for the moment that it were in Afghanistan).[1]

Finally, we have the experience of encountering maternity as a part of everyday life. A woman carries a child onto the bus or the airplane (and you mutter a devout prayer that the child will not be in the seat next to you and scream the whole trip), a baby flirts with you behind his mother's back in a supermarket; we see a mother attempting to protect her child from the horrors of war revealed in an ugly, painful scene on the evening TV news; a woman walks down the street pushing a baby buggy; we walk through an art gallery filled with Renaissance madonnas.

There are almost overwhelming emotional currents released by such encounters with maternity. We remember in the depths of our souls (unconsciously, perhaps) what it was like to be mothered, to be cared for, to be protected, to be loved. Indeed, much of the activities of our lives are driven by latent personality dynamisms which seek to recapture the security, the affection, the total care and concern which we experienced in infancy. We want someone to take care of us the way mother did—and not a few men marry the women they expect to be surrogate mothers, who will be their loving, devoted slaves for the rest of their lives.

Mothering is part of any intimate human relationship in the sense that we expect those who love us to be at least on occasion passionately tender toward us, to assume the responsibility of "taking care" of us. In marriage, then, a spouse does indeed mother the other, although for the emotional maturity and happiness of both, there ought to be other dimensions to their relationship too. There is no contradiction in saying that a husband must "mother" his wife on occasion. He is gentle and tender with her, "taking care" of her. One of the problems, of course, is that a man may not feel free to develop a sufficiently androgynous personality, and the feminine aspects of his selfhood atrophy; he is quite incapable of having any maternal dimension in his relationship with his wife. She may mother him—for her that comes relatively easily—but he may refuse to "mother" back, since for him, such behavior is quite difficult. The lack of symmetry in their marriage can be discouraging, frustrating, divisive.[2]

Mother love gets perverted in many cases. Women hate their children, use them, project their own frustrations and fantasies into them. Such are the tragic effects of human sinfulness. Still, anyone who has seen a new mother proudly carrying her child into church to be baptized knows that the biological-psychological thrust toward pride, tenderness, admiration, protection, reverence, and delight between a mother and a child is one of the most fundamental powers in the universe. There are some environmentalists and some feminists who have come to despise motherhood as a combination of oppression and pollution. I surely have no intention of arguing with people who hold such a viewpoint, although I must admit to being skeptical of the argument that holds that a woman's desire to have a child of her own to hold in her arms is culturally caused. I will cheerfully concede cultural conditioning; I will also concede that there are some women who do not want or are afraid to have a child. Still, I do not anticipate the time when even a majority of women will not feel proud of and passionately tender toward that strange, delightful, disturbing, and at times maddening combination of angel and devil they have brought into the world.

The primary element of sexual differentiation, then, is that women bear children and men do not. Women become mothers, men do not. (Men can act maternally, of course, and my assumption is that some maternal component in a man's personality enriches it rather than weakens it.) The experience of maternity, either in oneself or in someone else, is the core limit-experience of sexual differentiation. The mother gives life; she brings life into the world. The phenomenon of childbirth is commonplace; thousands of children are born every day. Birth need not be a limit-experience at all. (Although in research on mystical ecstasy done by William McCready and myself, the birth experience often triggers a mystical interlude—in fathers almost as often as mothers.)

That childbirth is an experience intimately related to religion is testified to by almost all the cultures humankind has ever known. For religion, of course, is concerned with the great mysteries of life and death, and in maternity one has the quintessence of the mystery of life. In the great religious image systems, the fertile womb of the mother is linked with both the container, the vessel, and with life-giving waters. It is not merely in the Book of Genesis that life springs from water. In almost all of the religions the world knows that out of water comes life, out of mother comes life.

Psychoanalysts are persuaded that in most dream symbolism water stands for the maternal womb. Indeed, the brilliant founder of the Chicago Institute of Psychoanalysis, the late Franz Alexander, wrote three volumes arguing just this point. In the world religions and in the human unconscious, then, water, mother, vessel, earth all converge to represent one life-containing, life-bestowing symbolism.[3]

The Great Mother is the primal goddess both psychologically and historically. The feminine aspect of the ultimate is the life-bestowing dimension of God as opposed to the life-ordering or masculine dimension. In most religions, creation represents an ordering of primal chaos rather than, as in the later Jewish and Christian view of things, the production of something out of nothing. In the pagan worldviews, life antedated creation, and it was the male deity or demiurge who slew the female dragon Chaos. Out of the parts of the slain primal chaos the male deity put together the ordered universe. If the female deity did indeed precede the male one in human cultic behavior, and the evidence from the caves suggest this, the reason was that our archaic predecessors thought of life as the raw, primal force that antedated any attempt to order and contain it, and that always threatened to erupt and break out of the ordinary compartments into which creation had placed it. The mother goddess, then, was the source of life, but the life force she gave was potentially destructive; it was raw, undisciplined, hard to contain. Humans had to tame that force by orderly cultivation of the fields and by domestication of the flocks. In some sense the human condition was a struggle to impose restraints and limitations on the raw power and vitality of the feminine life-giving force.

The Kagaba Indians describe it as well as anyone:

> The Mother of Songs, the mother of our whole seed, bore us in the beginning. She is the mother of all races of men and the mother of all tribes. She is the mother of the thunder, the mother of trees and of all kinds of things. She is the mother of songs and dances. She is the mother of the older brother stones. She is the mother of the grain and the mother of all things. She is the mother of the younger brother Frenchmen and of the strangers. She is the mother of the dance paraphernalia and of all temples, and the only mother we have. She is the mother of the animals, the only one, and the mother of the Milky Way. It was the mother herself who began to baptize. She gave us the limestone coca dish. She is the mother of the rain, the only one we have. She alone is the mother of things, she alone. And the mother has left a memory in all the temples. With her sons, the saviors, she left songs and dances as a reminder. Thus the priests, the fathers, and the older brothers have reported.
>
> Song of the Kagaba Indians, Colombia [4]

Isis in Egypt, Demeter in Greece, Juno in Rome, Ishtar in Phoenicia, Artemis in Archaic Ionia, Artargatis in Syria, Rati in Indonesia, Kali (in her more positive manifestations) in India, and such ambivalent Aztec earth goddesses as Tlazolteotl and Coatlicue in Mexico (both of whom, like Kali, were also death goddesses) have cousins all over the world.

One does not have to accept Neumann's Jungian psychology to agree with his summary of the role of the mother goddess in human religion:

> Thus the Feminine, the giver of nourishment, becomes everywhere a revered principle of nature, on which man is dependent in pleasure and pain. It is from this eternal experience of man, who is as helpless in his dependence on nature as the infant in his dependence on his mother, that the mother-child figure is inspired forever anew.
>
> This mother-child figure, then, does not betoken a regression to infantilism, in which an "adult" becomes a child, or is moved with nostalgia by the mother's love for her child; rather, man in his genuine identification with the child experiences the Great Mother as a symbol of the life on which he himself, the "grown-up," depends. [5]

When we move from pagan religions to Yahwism, the context changes dramatically. Eve is indeed the mother of us all, but she is not a goddess, she is an all-too-human earthbound person. The Eve of the Old Testament is probably a transformation and a humanization of a pre-Sinai Semitic mother goddess. The aim of the author of Genesis is obvious. Eve may represent the origin of human life; she may be the mother of us all; but she is not a goddess or a life force with specific power unto herself. She is rather a creature of Yahweh who gives life. Mary, too, is a human and a historical personage, a person who lived and died at a specific time in human history. She is not identified with the power of fertility, she is not the goddess who directs the raw, primal vitality inherent in reproduction of all life; she is the servant of the Lord, the agent of Yahweh. But it is still through her that Yahweh chooses to bring life to the world. She represents the rich, abundant, variegated creativity with which Yahweh has blessed the earth. Therefore she reveals to us the life-giving, the feminine dimension of Yahweh. She quite properly emerges as the Madonna, because she is a sacrament of Yahweh our loving Mother.

Christian poetry about Mary as Madonna, as Great Mother, is almost endless. Much of it is pretty bad, but from the fourth to the nineteenth centuries, Mary the Mother has inspired some of the finest poetry ever set on paper. Aurelius Clemens Prudentius tells us that she is the mother of a new age of golden life:

Sentisne, virgo nobilis,
Matura per fastidia
  Pudoris intactum decus
Honore partus crescere?

O quanta rerum gaudia
Alvus pudica continet,
  Ex qua novellum saeculum
Procedit et lux aurea!

Aurelius Clemens Prudentius
(348–413) Hymn XI of the
Cathemerinon, verses 53–60)

Know thou, O Virgin, noble-blest,
That through the timeless tunneled
  glooms
The blinding beauty of thy soul
With childbirth splendor flames and
  blooms?

What joys are fountained for the
  world
Within thy womb's well, deep and
  white,
Whence streams a new-created age
And golden light, and Golden Light!

(Translated from the Latin by Raymond F. Roseliep)

A thousand years later two anonymous bards sing the same song of praise:

> Mater, ora Filium,
> ut post hoc exilium
> nobis donet gaudium
> beatorum omnium!

Fair maiden, who is this Bairn,
That thou bearest on thine arm?
Sir, it is a King's Son,
That in heaven above doth wone.

Man to father hath he none,
But himself is God alone;
of a maid he would be born,
To save mankind that was forlorn.

The kings brought him presents,
Gold and myrrh and frankincense,
To my Son, full of might,
King of kings and Lord of right.

Fair maiden, pray for us
Unto thy Son, sweet Jesus,
That he will grant us of his grace
In heaven high to have a place!

"Fair Maiden, Who is This Bairn?"—Anonymous

Mary is a lady bright,
She hath a son of mickle might,
Over all this world she is light,
Bona natalicia.

Mary is so fair of face,
And her son so full of grace,
In Heaven (may) He make us a place,
Cum sua potencia.

Mary is so fair and bright,
And her son so full of might,
Over all this world He is light,
Bona voluntaria.

Mary is both good and kind,
Ever on us she hath mind,
That the fiend shall us not bind.
Cum sua malicia.

Mary is queen of everything,
And her son a lovely king;
God grant us all (a) good ending,
Regnat Dei gracia.

"Nunc Gaudet Maria"—Anonymous

Mary the Mother is called upon to help and protect us, to care for us as she cared for her son. The son was innocent and deserved her care; we have little reason to claim in right Mary's protection. We still plead for it. In the anguish of Geoffrey Chaucer, who was all too well aware of his own sinfulness:

And thou that art the flower of virgins all,
Of whom Bernard has such a love to write,
To thee now in beginning first I call!
Comfort of wretched us, help me recite
Thy maiden's death, who, through her merit bright,
Won life eternal, vanquishing with glory
The fiend, as men can read here in her story.

Thou daughter of thy son, mother and maid,
Thou well of mercy, sinful souls' physician,
In whom for goodness God to dwell essayed,
Thou humble, yet enthroned in high position,
So didst thou lift our nature with thy mission
That He that made all nature thus was won
To clothe in flesh and blood His only Son.

Within the blissful cloister of thy side
To man's shape grew the eternal Love and Peace,
Lord of the three-fold universe, and Guide,
Whom earth and heaven and ocean never cease
To praise, Thou, spotless virgin, for a space,
Bore in thee, maiden still in every feature,
He that Creator was of every creature.

In thee are mercy and magnificence,
Goodness and pity in such unity

That thou, that art the sun of excellence,
Not only helpest those that pray to thee,
But often times, in thy benignity,
Freely, before men any help petition,
Thou dost appear, and art their lives' physician.

Help me, thou lovely, meek, and blessèd maid,
Who banished now in bitterness must dwell;
Think on the wife of Canaan, she who said
That dogs would feed upon the crumbs that fell
Down from their master's table. I know well
that I am sinful, wretched son of Eve,
And yet accept my faith, for I believe.

And since all faith, when lacking works, is dead,
So give me now for work both wit and space.
That I from darkness be deliverèd!
O thou that art so fair and full of grace,
Be advocate for me in that high place
Where there is endless singing of "Hosannah!"
Mother of Christ, dear daughter of St. Anna!

And from thy light my soul in prison light,
Where it is troubled by contamination
Of this body, and the heavy weight
Of earthly lust, and all false inclination;
O heaven of refuge for us, O salvation
Of all souls whom distress and sorrow neighbor,
Help me, for I will now attempt my labor!

Invocatio Ad Mariam (From the Prologue to the Second Nun's Tale) by
Geoffrey Chaucer (Translated into Modern English by Frank Ernest Hill)

And that enigmatic son of the Renaissance, Desiderius Erasmus, turned to the Greek language that he helped restore to Europe to pray that the mother who brought life back to the world would free him from his sinfulness:

Hail, Jesus' Virgin-Mother ever blest,
Alone of women Mother eke and Maid,
Others to thee their several offerings make;
This one brings gold, that silver, while a third
Bears to thy shrine his gift of costly gems.

For these, each craves his boon—one strength of limb—
One wealth—one, through his spouse's fruitfulness,
The hope a father's pleasing name to bear—
One Nestor's eld would equal. I, poor bard,
Rich in goodwill, but poor in all beside,
Bring thee my verse—nought have I else to bring—
And beg, in quital of this worthless gift,
That greatest meed—a heart that feareth God,
And free for aye from sin's foul tyranny.
Erasmus, his vow.

"Votive Ode" (At Our Lady's Shrine in Walsingham)
(Translated from the Greek by J. T. Walford)

About the same time a much more simple poem was written in Spanish describing the marvelous events at Bethlehem:

White and crimson, cheek and breast,
O Virgin blest!
The pledge of love in Bethlehem
A flower was on the rose-tree's stem,
O Virgin blest!
In Bethlehem in sign of love
The rosebranch raised a rose above,
O Virgin blest!
In the rose came forth a flower—
Jesus, our high Lord of Power—
O Virgin blest!
The Rose of all the rosetree's span,
God in nature and a Man—
O Virgin blest!

"Cantiga" by Gil Vincente (1470–1540)
(Translated from the Galician-Castilian by Thomas Walsh)

Even the strange, half-mad Lord Byron could pause amidst his self-advertisements to wonder about the Madonna who brought life to the world:

Ave Maria! blessed be the hour!
The time, the clime, the spot, where I so oft
Have felt that moment in its fullest power
Sink o'er the earth so beautiful and soft,
While swung the deep bell in the distant tower,

Or the faint dying day-hymn stole aloft,
And not a breath crept through the rosy air,
And yet the forest leaves seem'd stirr'd with prayer.

Ave Maria! 'tis the hour of prayer!
  Ave Maria! 'tis the hour of love!
Ave Maria! may our spirits dare
  Look up to thine and to thy Son's above!
Ave Maria! oh that face so fair!
  Those downcast eyes beneath the Almighty Dove—
What though 'tis but a pictured image—strike?—
That painting is no idol, 'tis too like.

"Ave Maria" (From *Don Juan*, Canto III, cii, ciii)
by George Gordon, Lord Byron (1788–1824)

But of all the Madonna poems, my own favorite is that of the good nineteenth-century Jesuit, Gerard Manley Hopkins, who combined the simplicity of the medieval bards with the complex rhythms that astonish the most modern of poets.

May is Mary's month, and I
Muse at that and wonder why:
  Her feasts follow reason,
  Dated due to season—

Candlemas, Lady Day;
But the Lady Month, May,
  Why fasten that upon her,
  With a feasting in her honour?

Is it only its being brighter
Than the most are must delight her?
  Is it opportunest
  And flowers finds soonest?

Ask of her, the mighty mother:
Her reply puts this other
  Question: What is Spring?—
  Growth in every thing—

Flesh and fleece, fur and feather,
Grass and greenworld all together;
  Star-eyed strawberry-breasted
  Throstle above her nested

Cluster of bugle blue eggs thin
Forms and warms the life within;
And bird and blossom swell
In sod or sheath or shell.

All things rising, all things sizing
Mary sees, sympathising
With that world of good,
Nature's motherhood.

Their magnifying of each its kind
With delight calls to mind
How she did in her stored
Magnify the Lord.

Well but there was more than this:
Spring's universal bliss
Much, how much to say
To offering Mary May.

When drops-of-blood-and-foam-dapple
Bloom lights the orchard-apple
And thicket and thorp are merry
With silver-surfèd cherry

And azuring-over greybell makes
Wood banks and brakes wash wet like lakes
And magic cockoo call
Caps, clear, and clinches all—

This ecstasy all through mothering earth
Tells Mary her mirth till Christ's birth
To remember and exultation
In God who was her salvation.

"The May Magnificat" Gerard Manley Hopkins (1844–1889)

It seems to me that the essence of Mary as mother goddess, Mary as a sign of fertility, Mary as symbol of the raw, life-giving power of Yahweh is caught up in those lines, "What is Spring?—/ Growth in every thing—" It's all there—the raw, primal power of fertility, the awesome mystery of life, the elementary, biological fact of maternity, of nature's motherhood. In the poem it is embodied as "Flesh and fleece, fur and feather, Grass and green-

Ivory Madonna (anonymous)
—Courtesy of Musées Nationaux, Paris

Pietà (Michelangelo)—St. Peter's, Rome

Annunciation (Botticelli)—Uffizi, Florence

Three-spiral pattern
—New Grange, Ireland

Isis with Horus

Sardinian goddess
with young god

Tibetan Tara

Tondo Doni (Michelangelo)—Uffizi, Florence

Assumption of the Virgin (El Greco)
—Courtesy of The Art Institute of Chicago

Ériu—Jim Fitzpatrick © 1976

world all together," and all combine to proclaim the endless generation. Nature's motherhood, "All things rising, all things sizing/ Mary sees, sympathising" is part of Hopkin's Christian song, but he sings of an experience that goes back to the grotesque (to us) Venuses of our cave-dwelling predecessors. It is an experience that probably goes back to the dawn of mankind, to the time when a man was overwhelmed with astonishment at the sight of an infant in his woman's arms.

I would submit that the images of Hopkins, Byron, Chaucer, Erasmus, the nameless medieval bards, and the elegant Prudentius tell us far more about the power and the meaning of the Madonna than theology books could possibly portray. Poetry is much better at conveying limit-experience than scholarly theology.[6]

As for the Madonna in plastic art, one could argue until Judgment Day about which paintings were the best. I would walk through the whole Uffizi Gallery in Florence just to look at Michelangelo's *Holy Family on the Barrelhead.* Hans Memling's *Adoration of the Angels* in the Prado in Madrid, the fourteenth-century sculpture in the Notre Dame church in Riom, France; Donatello's relief in Turin, Leonardo da Vinci's *The Virgin and Saint Anne* in the Louvre, Van der Weyden's Flemish madonnas—all represent dimensions of motherhood. Some of them are very spiritual, some are very earthy; but all reflect the mystery of birth and of the passionate protective tenderness, the fierce dedication and devotion of a mother toward her child. While it is unfashionable now to be very enthusiastic about Raphael and Botticelli, the melancholy, reflective *Virgin with the Pomegranate* of Botticelli and the gentle serenity of Raphael's *Virgin with the Blue Veil* come mighty close to producing limit-experience in me every time I look at them, as does da Vinci's *Madonna of the Rocks.*

But when all is said and done, I still find myself back in the Uffizi looking at Michelangelo's *Holy Family.* The tender concern in the eyes, the playful pride in the slightly parted lips, the vigor of the body of the Virgin ever ready to hold and to protect the child. Oh, it's all larger than life, of course, and the Virgin may have an arm muscle to frighten Mohammed Ali; but she is a mother you wouldn't mess with. No one is ever going to hurt that child while she's around.

The strength of the Michelangelo madonna, the ever-so-slight satisfaction on the Virgin's face as she looks at the child against her breast in the Van der Weyden painting, the thoughtful, almost melancholy reflection on mystery in the Botticelli paintings, the fascination in Raphael's blue-veiled mother with her sleeping child, the mystic rapture of da Vinci's mother of the rocks, the life-giving mother of Prudentius, the sin-forgiving mother of Erasmus and Chaucer, the warm but distant mother of Lord Byron, and Hopkin's Mary—the sympathetic onlooker of the rebirth of nature in May—are just a handful of the images and pictures of Mary the Madonna that emerge from Christian art and poetry.[7] Irrelevant for our time? Well, maybe, but then so much the worse for our time.

What is the human existential need with which maternity as illumined by Mary seeks to dialogue? Just as maternity represents the most fundamental and primal and vital of life-giving forces, so existential anxiety, the fear of sickness unto death, is the most primal and elementary of human fears. Maternity means life; anxiety and fear mean death. Maternity is a response to despair. Indeed, in the poems of Byron, Chaucer, and Erasmus cited above, the wrestling with despair becomes quite explicit. Even in Hopkins, the celebration of May can only come from one who has already lived through the darkness of December.

In the Madonna we encounter the dilemma, the ambiguity, and the conflict between life and death. We know the Madonna's child will die, as will the child of every mother, even our own. We move dangerously close to despair. What point is there in life if it is all to be snuffed out in death? Is there no purpose? No love? No grace? Is this surging creativity to be blotted out in oblivion? Are the life-producing forces to be routed ultimately by the life-destroying forces? Can we respond to life only with a brave, stoic despair?

Our perceptions have been caught in the hardened, rigid structure of the common defeats in life—discouragement, frustration, sickness, old age, death. And then we encounter maternity as illumined by the Madonna. We can glance over the lines of the poetry that extols her and walk quickly by the paintings that portray her and nothing will happen. But once the existential need for meaning has become powerful (and that may never happen), we may stop to read, we may stop to look, and we may pause to reflect on our own experience of woman as mother. We become aware of the overwhelming power of life; we think of the surge of fertility each year in the spring, of "flesh and fleece, fur and feather,/ Grass and greenworld all together." Doubtless there is death and destruction all through the world, doubtless we shall die; but here is maternity, fertility, birth, life, rebirth. We are now up against the limits of our own existence, the horizon of our own being; but we also perceive life, and we perceive it as a gift, a given, as something wildly, madly, exuberantly gratuitous. "All things rising, all things sizing."

What is one to make of this "ecstasy all through mothering earth"? It is grace; it claims to reveal; it claims to be a sacrament of something else. It is a gift. Might there possibly be a Giver, a Giver of whom fertility, maternity, even the lovely-eyed Madonna are but a pale reflection? Can it be so? Might it be so? Is it so? Is there passionate, life-giving tenderness out there beyond the horizon of our life?

If we have been sufficiently captured by maternity-turned-symbol, by the grace that the Madonna as sacrament has revealed to us, then we can begin to hope once again. The shattered structures of our perceptions are organized around a symbol which has captured our experience of rebirth. "Life and Death are inseparable on earth for they are 'twain yet one and death is birth." [8] The symbol takes possession of us; our perceptions are restructured, and we begin to move.

Where do we move? Well, we move to the earth that is the source of the gift of life. We commit ourselves to bringing joy and happiness and peace and love to the earth. If we are followers of the Madonna, there is no room for despair, no room for hopelessness, no room to give up or quit. Servants of Mary who have committed themselves to political and social reform do not withdraw from the contest when the going gets tough and when they suffer repeated setbacks. They do not despair because the Enlightenment-socialist dreams have turned into nightmares, they do not seek stoic gods like Atlas to wait bravely for the end, they refuse to listen to the prophets of doom; they set out to build and rebuild with no fear for the ultimate outcome. Their hope is not based on economic projections, political assessments, computer models, or ideological convictions. It is based on their faith that the earth is graceful, that the world is gracious, that it is a given, a gift, a reflection of a Giver who is as tender and gentle, as passionate and as generous as the Madonna.

The followers of Mary do not, heaven save us, abandon economics, politics, planning, projections, or even computer models, but they find in them neither the source of their faith nor the depth of their commitment. Their faith is not rooted in social science or social ideology but in a vision of a world animated by the passionate, life-giving tenderness of which the Madonna is a sacrament.

Is that the way things really are? Is the ultimate really the kind of life-giving love that is reflected in the Madonna? A cautious world says probably not; the followers of Mary have made the opposite choice.

It is but a step from saying that the life-giving power of earth symbolized as life-giving love in Mary reflects the life-giving love of the ultimate to assert further that the earth is Mary's garden. Such a symbolic and poetic statement merely means that the earth is a sacrament; it is sacred and must be treated with reverence and respect and awe and a sense of mystery. If the earth is Mary's garden, you don't rip it up or rip it off. Respect for the physical environment is not just a new notion dug up to give relevance to an outmoded symbol that one is trying to rehabilitate for the modern world. Respect for the environment, on the contrary, is at the very core of the Mary myth—though the phrase "respect for environment" is new. If "all things rising" reflect through Mary the life-giving love of God, then all the rising things on earth are mystery. To pollute, abuse, corrupt, destroy these things is a sacrilege.

You cannot have a successful environmental movement unless you restore a sense of reverence and awe to the human community. If the cosmos is a machine or a set of mathematical formulae or an empty collection of random atoms, then why should we respect it or reverence it? Why should we not exploit it to the fullest? Why should we worry about what or who comes after us? Everything will be wiped out in nothingness eventually, so why not take what we can get now? This is not a very noble way of thinking, but it is a very human way. Most of the ecological enthusiasts, captives of the Enlightenment still, seem to think you can respect the environment without reverencing it, that you can have concern about the environment without seeing any mystery in it. Guilt and fear are their two primary weapons, because that is all they have to motivate people. The cosmos has been drained of mystery and of the sacred. For some, environmental concern can become an ideological movement that serves as a substitute for religion. Fine for them, but most of humankind will respect the earth again only when they see it once more as a park, a paradise given to them by God but still belonging to him. The earth will be Mary's garden or a trash heap.

The Mary myth is not the only one that can provide a restructuring of perceptions and illumination and direction to respond to the critical issues of our day. There may well be other symbols that work just as well or perhaps even better. Still, if we are going to save the earth, it damn well better become someone's garden.

As we try to sort out the meaning of masculinity and femininity in an era that is rethinking sex roles, Mary may well be the best available argument for the androgynous personality, the personality that combines the essence of each sex. For if God is androgynous—and that's what the mother goddesses reveal to us—then it is all right for humankind to be androgynous. In principle, almost any one of the female deities could underwrite the upgrading of women. There is no particular reason why it has to be Mary. But she is the only mother goddess currently available. Astarte, Lilith, Demeter, Isis, Ishtar, Nut, Kali, Coatlicue, Rati, Ceres, Tlazoltoatl—that crowd—are not around much these days. You might not like Mary particularly, but if you want someone to convey the idea that God is androgynous, she is about all you have (unless you want to return to the mother goddesses of witchcraft, which not a few people seem to be doing).

G. K. Chesterton finds in Mary the appeal of hearth and home and the traditional wisdom of the fields:

> The dark Diana of the groves
>   Whose name is Hecate in hell
> Heaves up her awful horns to heaven
>   White with the light I know too well.
>
> The moon that broods upon her brows
>   Mirrors the monstrous hollow lands
> In leprous silver; at the term
>   Of triple twisted roads she stands.
>
> Dreams are no sin, or only sin
>   For them that waking dream they dream;
> But I have learned what wiser knights
>   Follow the Grail and not the Gleam.
>
> I found One hidden in every home,
>   A voice that sings about the house,
> A nurse that scares the nightmares off,
>   A mother nearer than a spouse,
>
> Whose picture once I saw; and there
>   Wild as of old and weird and sweet,
> In sevenfold splendour blazed the moon
>   Not on her brow; beneath her feet.

"The White Witch" G. K. Chesterton, *The Queen of Seven Swords*

For women, Mary symbolizes the awesome power of femininity. To be a woman does not mean to be quiet, retiring, weak, diffident, inferior; it means to be strong, powerful, creative, dynamic. One can afford to be tender, gentle, loving, caring because one knows that these are not signs of weakness, that they can coexist with aggressive, strong, outgoing, directive behavior. If Mary reflects an androgynous God, femininity is as good as masculinity.

And if there is nothing weak or effeminate about life-giving love, about maternal love that is both passionately tender and fiercely protective, there is no reason why a man must retreat behind the shield of hypermasculinity; he can afford to be tender, sympathetic, caring because Mary reveals to him that these qualities are signs not of weakness but of strength. If God can be tender and passionate, if God is reflected by Mary as a source of maternal life-giving love, then the tender, gentle man is not weak but strong. In the God who is revealed to us in Mary, masculine and feminine are blended. Among the followers of Mary, sharp, exclusive, and oppressive distinctions between men and women are not appropriate. As Professor Robert Higham has pointed out, the sharp demarcation line between men and women, against which the feminist movement is quite properly revolting, is a relatively modern development, a product of the Enlightenment passion for clear and sharp distinctions. Women did not lead armies into battle in the Crimean War. (They certainly couldn't have done any worse than the male generals did.) Nor can one imagine cathedrals being built to women in the France and England of the nineteenth century.

I am not suggesting that traditional Marian theory or piety anticipated the feminist movement. Nor am I denying that corrupt Mariology has been used by some people in the Roman Church to underwrite the most benighted and oppressive attitudes toward the role of woman. The *Kirche und Kinder* view of women was far more appropriate for a pre-Christian peasant society than it is for Christianity. That so many Christians mouthed it and distorted Marian imagery to support it is a sign of how strong and persistent has been the worldview of peasant paganism (which bubbled to the surface with terrifying horror in the Nazi movement in Germany).

But the feminist movement today is hardly derived from older Marian theory, at least not in any explicit sense (though a case could be made that Christianity developed a culture through the Mary symbol in which feminism could emerge eventually). I am content with a much more modest statement: the high tradition of Mariology is compatible with a theory of the role of women which emphasizes the freedom, independence, strength, passion, and responsibility of maternity. It is less compatible with one that emphasizes the quiet, docile, retiring, passive, fragile role of woman that was so dear to both the Victorians and the Nazis, as well as to some of the fertility cultists of the Catholic

Church of not so long ago who seemed to believe that the number of children one had was a measure of how well one had discharged maternal functions and responsibilities.

The argument needs only to be minimal. There is reinforcement in the Mary myth for both environmental concern and feminism, and there is no consolation at all in the myth for those who do not care about the environment or who want to keep women in dependent positions. Indeed, the thought of a follower of Mary being dependent would be funny were it not that so many people badly misunderstand the Mary myth and think of her as weak and passive. They know nothing of the origins of the maternal symbol in religion and understand little of it in their own religion. In fact, the symbol stands for massive, awesome, life-giving strength, a strength that is combined with fierce protectiveness and passionate tenderness which reflect a God strong enough to be tender and passionate enough to overwhelm us with his/her life-giving love.

What is the world all about? What is the nature of everything? Is it an idiot's tale, random chance, a plot? If it is a plot, what is the plotter like? It cannot be a romance or a tender love story—or can it? The person who wrote one of the earliest extant poems to Mary in the English language thought it was, and a mother was at the heart of the story.

> Be glad in heart, grow great before the Lord
> for thy comfort, and build up glory;
> hold thy hoard locked, bind fast thy thought
> in thine own mind. Many a thing is unknown.
> True comrades sometimes fall away, tired,
> word-promises grow faint; so fares this world,
> going swiftly in showers, shaping its destiny.
> There is one faith, one living Lord,
> one Baptism, one Father everlasting,
> one Lord of peoples who made the world,
> its good things and joys. Its glory grew
> through this passing earth, stood for a long time
> hidden in gloom, under a dark helm,
> well screened by trees, overshadowed by darkness,
> till a brave-hearted maid grew up among mankind.
> There it pleased Him who shaped all life,

the Holy Ghost,   to dwell in her treasure-house—
bright on her breast   shone the radiant Child
who was the beginning   of all light.

"A Brave-Hearted Maid"
from the Old English by Margaret Williams

MADONNA

Experience of Sexual Differentiation	Maternity
Biological Origin	Birth, nursing, taking care
Cognate Symbols	Earth, water (womb), home, hearth
Ancient Goddesses	Isis, Demeter, Juno
Type	Eve, the source of life
Mary Symbol	Madonna
Existential Need	Discouragement, despair
Limit-Experience	Vitality of cosmos, life-giving love
Grace that is Given	Inexhaustible and passionate tenderness of life-giving love
Illumination—Restructuring of Perceptions	Hope
Action	Protection and improvement of the earth (Mary's garden)
Man-Woman Implication	Acceptance of androgyny
Poem	"May Magnificat" (Hopkins)
Plastic Art	*Holy Family* of Michelangelo

Part III

VIRGO

HYMN TO MY FAVORITE THREE-YEAR-OLD

Surely, leprechaun child, a mistaken name
What 'tween you and the frenzied queen of old.
Giant blue eyes, curly red hair, winsome smile
A perfect little lady in every way
Sweet, lovely, innocent
Charming all who cross the stage
The pride of the nineteenth ward
The inestimable Nora Maeve.

Who can resist your grin
Who imagine the slightest temper
Who deny your smallest whim
But let them try
And they'll have their lunch
They'll see the fiery, the frenzied
The inextinguishable Nora Maeve.

No need to fight,
Conflict quite beside the point
We'll do it my way, of course
Pleasant, reasonable, cooperative
Who can possibly disagree
        with sensible Nora Maeve.

Shape up world, get your act in line
Ready or not, here she comes
And take it from us
She'll accept none of your guff
'Tis time to prepare the way
Here comes the imperial and imperious Nora Maeve.

Enough of your nonsense, disordered cosmos
No more loafing on the job, guardian spirits
Let's get this show on the road
Fagablough, look out, here she is!
Hell on wheels, pretty Nora Maeve.

Mommy and daddy, Liam and Andy, Sebi too
And all the rest of you
To receive your orders get in line
All hail her High Mightiness
The grand duchess Nora Maeve.

And God up in heaven
'Twas your idea, after all
You who renew the human race
     through girl children such as she
Maybe you're ready for her
If so, 'twill be a better world
And in years to come they'll chant her praise
And we'll say, oh yes, we knew her when
The famous, the saintly Nora Maeve.

                                        A. M. G.

Chapter 6

VIRGO
ATQUE SEMPER VIRGO

T he symbol of Mary as Virgin is the hardest of all to explore in the modern world. Part of the problem comes from misunderstanding the symbol. It is, as we said in Chapter 4, part of a limit-language paradox, Virgin Mother. It is *not* a symbol of sexual "purity" or repression. At least in its origins and in its high tradition, the Virgin symbol represents renewal, transformation, the beginning of a new creation. Unfortunately for all too many Catholics raised in the last fifty years, Mary's virginity speaks not of the transformation of humankind but of measurements of hemlines and necklines, of singing "Mother Beloved" at the beginning of a high school prom, and of a whole range of detailed sexual prohibitions and restrictions. Mary's virginity was equated with frigidity for all practial purposes, particularly in the more recent northern European Catholic tradition and especially (God forgive us for it) among the Irish Catholics.[1]

The symbol of woman as positive transforming force, which is deeply rooted in most religious traditions and, if we are to believe the Jungians, also firmly embedded in the human unconscious, is not easily understood in a modern world which worships orgasm as the only meaningful sexual interchange. Curiously enough, the gonadal determinism involved in orgasm worship is justified in terms of the sexual liberation allegedly made possible by Freudian psychoanalysis. Freud, of course, had

133

a much more differentiated and nuanced view of human sexuality, but the distance between the real Freud and the pop Freudianism which sees orgasm as the only self-fulfilling expression of sex is a very great distance indeed.

Nevertheless, most relationships between men and women do not culminate in genital sexuality. A mother, a daughter, a professional colleague, a friend can all be strong feminine influences in the life of a man without there being any genital sexuality involved. Furthermore, even two people who have intercourse together are not—save in the fantasy world of *Playboy* and *Penthouse*—making love all the time. There are nongenital interludes and episodes in their lives which occupy far more time than those periods they spend in bed with one another. While the influence a woman has on her man in facilitating the growth and transformation and renewal of his personality is linked with lovemaking, it is also distinct from it and persists even when intercourse becomes impossible for one reason or another (physical separation, for example).

Such observations are so obvious that they almost do not need to be made except for the fact that the current fixation on orgasmic satisfaction (understandable, perhaps, after a long era of puritanism) seems to make it impossible for many people to consider any other dimension of human sexuality.

A serious literary exception is Gabriel Fielding's little noticed but brilliant novel, *Gentlemen in Their Season.*[2] Bernard Persage, the hero, has a wife, a mistress, and a friend. The first presides over the cozy, reassuring domesticity of his home and family, the second leads him off to Calais on a great love affair which doesn't quite work out, and the third—a lutanist, composer, and an intellectual—is the only one of the three to whom he can talk. Most of the reviewers of the book could not understand the relationship between Persage and the friend, Emily Link; but surely such a refusal to understand was caused by ideological blinders. If Bernard had gone to bed with Emily, it would fit the conventional wisdom of pop Freudianism. For her to remain a transforming influence in his life—as common as such friendships may be in the real world—is still an affront to orgasm worship.

Yet the transforming influence of the opposite sex is an obvious datum of ordinary life. A woman comes into a room where there are a group of men. The language changes, the conversation becomes more impressive, and the competitive behavior among the males to make an impression noticeably increases. The ideologues of the woman's movement will argue, of course, that the change in language and conversational subject is sexist, and that if women were permitted into the same life-situations as men, conversations full of vulgarity and obscenity would continue undiminished with the appearance of a woman. Surely in some occupational and social situations where such liberated women are present, such transformations of language and conversation will not happen. Indeed, when a woman is present the men may compete not so much to elevate the language as to make it even coarser. Familiarity may breed contempt, and so much the better the movement would argue.

In fact, all the feminist ideology in the world will not change the propensity of members of one sex to try to impress members of the other. No man likes to lose a tennis match while women are watching. He is humiliated. The presence of women— perhaps a special woman—in the audience motivates him to try much harder to win (unless, of course, he is a tennis pro whose motivation for victory is quite independent of the sexual composition of the audience). Nor will all the feminist ideology in the world ever bring about a situation in which it makes no difference to the average golfer whether he tees off in front of a mixed audience or not. If there are women present, there is no way he will not try harder. (And alas, the game of golf being the diabolic enterprise it is, he is thereby much more likely to make a fool of himself and slice the ball three fairways away.)

This desire to impress a member of the opposite sex is quite unrelated to whether one is sleeping with him/her or not. A man wants to impress his wife every bit as much as he wants to impress a strange woman or a woman he is courting. It is a normal human response to try to impress a person. We want the other to like us, to approve of us, to admire us. If the stranger happens to be a member of the opposite sex, we simply try harder. Obviously such an urge to impress is rooted ultimately in the radical possibility of having intercourse with the other person, but normally intercourse will not occur, and is not even a remote possibility in the minds of the people involved. The presence of a member of the opposite sex heightens our consciousness and transforms our behavior quite independently of how honorable our intentions may be.

The consolation of a tender nurse when one is sick, the efficiency of a coolly competent assistant or associate when one is in the midst of confusion, the reassurance of a mother or a sister or a daughter when one is lonely or confused, the laughter of a friend at a party when one is distressed or depressed are all examples of the transforming and renewing impact of sexual differentiation. In a happy marriage, the wife plays all these roles— nurse, organizer, mother, mistress, daughter, provider of comic relief.[3] Lovemaking between husband and wife integrates all these other and transforming dimensions of their relationship. Yet, over the long haul in their marriage, it is precisely their ability to use sexual differentiation as an occasion for a mutual transforming and renewing experience that will condition the payoff each receives from genital sexuality.

The experience of the transforming power of sexual differentiation is universal. (Or as the dean of students remarked in the seminary—as close to an all-male world in the 1940s as one could imagine—"after a while, you begin to imagine that you hear the click of heels on the sidewalk.") This transforming power is biologically rooted. A member of the opposite sex "arouses" us. In many circumstances the physical arousal is slight or virtually nonexistent, but the psychological arousal remains and persists. In that arousal, our consciousness is heightened and our behavior is transformed either dramatically or very little, but enough so that we are aware of the potential for transformation and renewal.

However difficult it may be to sell the notion of woman as a source of transformation, inspiration, and renewal to the modern world, this aspect of sexual differentiation was obvious to our archaic ancestors. The gate, the tomb, the central pillar of the house, the enclosure, the cattle pen, the village, the city, and ultimately the nation were conceived of as female in nature. As Neumann says:

The woman is the natural nourishing principle and hence mistress of everything that implies nourishment. The finding, composition, and preparation of food, as well as the fruit and nut gathering of the early cultures, are the concern of the female group. Only the killing of large animals falls to the males, but the life and fertility of the animals were subordinated to the Feminine, since hunting magic, the magical guarantee of success in the hunt, lay in her province, although it was later taken over by the male hunting group. This rule over food was largely based on the fact that the female group formed the center of the dwelling, i.e., the actual home to which the nomadic males again and again returned.[4]

The woman, then, is primordially the natural, nourishing principle, the mistress of all that implies nourishment—house, table, hearth, and bed. She is responsible, of course, for physical transformation, for the cooking, the maintenance of the house, those primal activities of transforming the world. In the Roman mythology, there was even an oven goddess, Fornacalia, on whose feast day the national bread was baked. An old Roman proverb announced, "The oven is the mother."

Moreover, the woman had charge of the medicines, and so the feminine deity who was already responsible for the crops, the herds, and the fruit became the numinous agent in charge of curatives, intoxicants, and poisons. The woman, according to Neumann, learned the mysterious powers of fermentation and intoxication as the gatherer and storer of plants and herbs. From this wisdom it was but a step for the woman, and the goddess experience through her, to become the shaman, the sibyl, the priestess, and the wise woman. Woman became the "manna" figure, the Ceres, the lady of the wisdom bringing waters from the depths of the murmuring aspects of the fountain. Then, in one more step, the female goddesses of transformation emerged as the nymphs, the wood spirits, and finally, the graces and the muses.

Indeed, Neumann argues that the notion of a virgin-mother goddess is by no means unique or original to Christianity. It is the son of the virgin mother who renews the earth:

> The childbearing virgin, the Great Mother as a unity of mother and virgin, appears in a very early period as the

virgin with the ear of grain, the heavenly gold of the stars, which corresponds to the earthly gold of the wheat. This golden ear is a symbol of the luminous son who on the lower plane is borne as grain in the earth and in the crib, and on the higher plane appears in the heavens as the immortal luminous son of night. Thus the virgin with the spica, the ear of grain, and the torchbearer, Phosphora, are identical to the virgin and the child.[5]

It would be a mistake to push Neumann's insight too far, for there is obviously substantial differences between the transforming and renewing virgin mother of the fertility cults and the transforming virgin mother of Christianity, but the idea is not completely foreign to the human religious tradition (which does *not* necessarily mean that the Christian theme of the virgin mother is a symbol without any grounding in actual historical event).

The mother goddess as a source of manna, the source of spiritual transformation, reaches her height of development in the figure of Sophia, or Wisdom, in late antiquity. She is not abstract, disinterested knowledge but rather the wisdom that comes from loving participation. As Neumann puts it: "Just as the unconscious reacts and responds, just as the body reacts to healthful food or poison, so Sophia is living and present and near, a godhead that can always be summoned and is always ready to intervene, and not a deity living inaccessible to man in numinous remoteness and alienated seclusion." [6] Neumann notes that the Christian figure of the Madonna sheltering humanity under her mantle corresponds rather neatly with this late pagan notion of Sophia. And of course Beatrice is Sophia transformed and personalized in Dante's *Divine Comedy*.[7]

The spiritual mother or the virgin mother, the Sophia of the pagans, is indeed the mother goddess of earlier antiquity; but, as well as being the agent of transforming others, she has been transformed herself. She communicates now not so much a life of earthbound materiality as a life of the spirit. She is interested not merely in reproduction and in caring for the child but also in the whole man through the whole process of his spiritual development. In Buddhism, Kwan-yin is the transforming mother; in

India, Shakti and even Kali, in her benign manifestation, becomes a spiritual mother; and in Yoga, Tara—the One Who Leads Happily Across—is the spiritual mother (complete with the lotus and the lily which symbolize spiritual transformation).

Old paganism, then, saw the goddess as the source of transformation, mostly that transformation that came from drugs and intoxicants. Later paganism reconceptualized the transforming mother as a spiritual force, calling forth the highest and the most noble in the creative powers of human beings—though that did not necessarily exclude the use of drugs and intoxicants. The sibyl or the seer frequently uttered her wisdom under the influence of narcotics.

The moon, the gentle, numinous orb in the sky at night, became the natural symbol of the transforming goddess, as did the lotus and the lily and sometimes the tree. The goddess of transformation was perhaps a fertility goddess in her origin, but she became one of spiritual transformation, of wisdom, of human renewal as the years went on.

Mary, the Virgin "full of grace," is not discontinuous from the transforming mother, the wisdom-giving virgin of the world religions. She is the spiritual mother, the mother who consoles, protects, watches over her children not merely in physical infancy and childhood but throughout the course of their spiritual development. For her to be full of grace does not primarily describe the state of her own spirituality; it means that she is full of graciousness *for us*. As the virgin mother, the renewing and transforming woman pours over us the renewing waters of graciousness. The virgin mother is the mother who *cares*.

The human existential need, which opens us up to the limit-experience of woman as inspiration, transformation, and renewal, is the limit-experience of weariness. It is related to the experience of death anxiety described in the previous chapter but distinct from it. When we are weary "in the middle course of life" (as Dante has put it), or indeed at any other course of life, it is impossible to surmount the ennui of routine, monotony, mediocrity, ordinariness, the mundaneness of our life. The sheer boredom of our everyday life drags us down into a rut from which it seems impossible to get out. "Oh, weary, weary is the world." Our vitality is spent, our exuberance is gone, our creative energies are exhausted; the muse (literally, in this case) no longer speaks to us. There seems no point in trying because everything we do is doomed to failure. It is at this stage of the game that we are open to renewing experiences in the sense that we desperately need such experiences. We may fall in love—wisely or not—or fall back into love again as we rediscover (perhaps for the first time) our old love. We may be caught in a numinous experience, perhaps one of ecstasy, which draws us up out of ourselves, renewed, reinvigorated, transformed. Mary, the virgin mother, is the Christian symbol that illuminates our weariness, our discouragement, our frustration, and draws us in tenderly and compassionately to an experience which inspires and transforms us, gives us new life. She is the virgin mother presiding over our rebirth, just as in the birth of Jesus she presided over the rebirth of humanity.

What is it about Being that is revealed to us in these limit-experiences of transformation, which run the full range from falling in love to mystical ecstasy? When the thing becomes a symbol and in that becoming renews us, what is the grace that is given? What is the insight that is provided? The virgin mother as renewing sacrament—what aspect of the androgynous deity does she reflect upon us?

The renewal experience is essentially an experience of fidelity. Ecstatic, mystical experiences are brief, numinous instants in which we see the whole purpose of the universe converging, and we see our place in it. It all *does* make sense; there *is* a purpose; there *are* promises which are being kept. That which in a limit-experience is revealed as life-giving love through the madonna aspect of the Mary symbol is now revealed as faithful love, love with plan and purpose, love which does not repent of the promises it has made, love which draws us up out of ourselves and integrates us into its dazzling unity, love which bathes us with joy, serenity, peace, confidence, and sometimes even literally heat and light. After such an experience, weariness and discouragement are no longer possible; we have been transformed precisely because the old structures of perception trapped us in the mud and mire of weariness and randomness, and they have been reintegrated into a new structure of confidence. Before the experience, everything seemed random, loose, unintegrated. There was no animating spirit at work—no wisdom, no sense in the casual, disordered phenomena of our life. Now, after the experience, we have a whole new constellation of perceptions in which we see purpose animated by gentle and powerful love, and we see ourselves integrated into that purpose. To love life is not purposeless, aimless, useless; not unintelligent, not blind; it is rather directed, purposeful, concerned, involved with us.

One need not undergo such an ecstatic experience of the numinous to be renewed, inspired, transformed. Nor need the limit-experience be a shattering once-and-for-all event, for there is transformation and renewal in everyday life. It need not necessarily be associated with sexual differentiation, though that is indeed a powerful and important occasion for transformation and renewal. A gentle breeze at the end of a hot day, a rain shower at the end of a dry summer, the first warm breath of spring after months of cold, the smile on a child's face when we come home after a hard day's work, a kind word from someone we have helped are all revelatory of the existence of a reality that is "full of grace." The Mary symbol deepens, enriches, reinforces, and illuminates these episodes of transformation and rebirth that are available to us in our everyday life, if only we are willing to pause to consider them. It is not all vain and purposeless. Our efforts are not wasted; we are reborn, we can start again.

The illumination that invades our personality in the restructuring of our perception in the limit-experience of spiritual transformation is the illumination of trust. One can trust the cosmos because the cosmos and the purpose behind it are reflected to us in the transforming experience of the protective, revitalizing virgin mother. If one can trust the ultimate, if one can trust the universe, if one can trust life, then one can trust one's fellow humans—not naïvely, not innocently, not without caution and sophistication certainly, but it is not necessary any longer to cut oneself off in alienation, isolation, fearful cynicism and suspicion. You can risk yourself in relationships with others because even if you get hurt, the tender virgin mother, reflecting the tender, renewing God, will drape her great blue mantle around you in protection. Your heart may break if you risk yourself in trust; Mary will put the pieces back together again.

This is not merely sentiment. Mary protecting us under her mantle is an image that reflects the protective power of life-giving, life-renewing love. To believe in the virgin mother's protective mantle is to believe in love. To dismiss that protective mantle as a meaningless, sentimental image is to reject the notion that there is life-renewing love at work in the cosmos. One may not like the imagery of the virgin's mantle, of course, but one must recognize that such imagery is rooted in the sacred Scriptures, persistent throughout the whole Christian religion, virtually universal in the more developed forms of paganism, and, if we are to believe the Jungians, rooted in the depths of the human unconscious—or, if we prefer Eliade, rooted in the structure of common human experience. Dispense with Mary's blue mantle, if you wish, but understand that it is a powerful image of the protective power of the transforming goddess.

If it is possible to trust, then it is possible to make commitments which are permanent and which will not be withdrawn when one grows weary, frustrated, and discouraged. These commitments can be made to other human beings, particularly to a spouse, parents, children. They can be made to friends, organizations, careers, vocations. One does not abandon a career or a vocation merely because one is tired of it—at least not if one is open to the limit-experience of spiritual transformation.[8]

One can also make commitments to causes not out of immaturity but out of maturity, not out of weakness but out of strength, not out of fear but out of confidence, not out of suspicion and hatred but out of trust and love. When the cause for which one stands receives frustration, setback, failure—as do all causes—then one has the resourcefulness, the resilience, the strength to bounce back and start over. He who has been through a decisive limit-experience of transformation and renewal knows that quitting is a luxury he cannot afford and an escape he does not want. Mary, the inspiring, transforming, renewing virgin mother, from whom came the Christian worldview—the most decisive of renewal experiences, the rebirth of humankind—incarnates and symbolizes the human capacity to be transformed and renewed and the divine love at work in the world striving to transform and renew our troubled, battered, weary souls when we are caught in the frustrations and discouragements of "the middle course of life," whenever that middle course might be.

One can reject the possibility of renewal; one can deny that there is any transforming, inspiring force at work in the universe. Then the virgin mother full of grace will seem a deceptive and foolish symbol. But if you do reject the virgin mother, reject her on the grounds that you do not believe in the possibility of renewal and transformation, that you do not believe in a life-restoring, life-transforming love at work in the universe. Reject Mary because you believe that weariness is the revelation of things the way they really are, that suspicion and cynicism are more appropriate responses to the human condition than trust and commitment. These are very plausible grounds for dismissing Mary full of grace as a relevant, outmoded, and deceptive symbol. But do not dismiss her because of what some nun told you in grammar school about patent leather shoes or low necklines, or what some priest preached to you at retreat about "impure thoughts." Do not dismiss her as a frigid, negative sex goddess; do not dismiss her as a fertility idol demanding from you as many children as possible. Do not dismiss her in the name of a pop Freudianism which believes that orgasmic satisfaction is the only thing in sex that really matters. None of these false images of Mary or oversimplified bits of conventional wisdom have anything to do with what the virgin mother full of grace really stands for. Men and women who are striving to work out their relationships at a time when sex roles are being reexamined can see the virgin mother as a by no means irrelevant religious symbol, for she stands as a rock-hard sign that transformation, rebirth, renewal is possible in a human life and in a human relationship.

Under normal circumstances, a renewal experience of sufficient power to shatter our weariness and restore our confidence in the fidelity of Being will come out of our marriage relationship. If a man cannot inspire and renew his wife and if a wife cannot renew and inspire her husband, then renewal and inspiration will not be likely for either of them. Some relationships have deteriorated so badly that there is simply nothing left. In others, there was nothing to begin with, and in still others the psychological incapacities of one or both partners are such that the relationship cannot become one of renewal or rebirth without major and lengthy psychotherapy at least. Still, we cannot sit around waiting for the numinous to invade our personalities in a full-blown ecstatic experience; nor can we expect that the casual love affair, for all its exciting and invigorating promise, will really do anything more than divert us from the weariness and discouragement of our lives. In ordinary circumstances, renewal is not to be found elsewhere—in another lover, another job, a trip to the Orient, or an interlude in a monastery (Buddhist or Christian). It is normally to be found by seeking the transforming and renewing elements in one's present environment. One of the most lamentable aspects of the human condition is that we carry our psychic environments with us. Everywhere we go becomes eventually just like the place before. Whatever love we have becomes eventually very like the last one.

Husbands and wives in the "middle course of life" remain skeptical about the possibility of change, renewal, transformation. Cynicism, suspicion, sophistication (usually of the pseudo variety) all lead them to ridicule the notion that anything can change in their relationship. It is absurd and foolish to think that there is even the faintest trace of potential for rebirth and renewal. Things are what they are and they are what they are going to be; nothing can change them. The woman has long since abandoned any notion of inspiring her husband. She is content to coexist, to accept, and to nag intermittently (or perhaps interminably). The husband expects no inspiration from his relationship with his wife. All the mystery, allure, and fascination has gone out of her. He takes her for granted. She is commonplace, ordinary, part of the environment. There may be no conflict of magnitude, no tensions which threaten to destroy the relationship, but nothing much exciting is left in it either, and both have become indignant and perhaps even angry at the suggestion that there was any possibility of transformation, inspiration, romance, mystery, discovery, adventure in their relationship. To inspire one's spouse, to renew and to restore, to give oneself over to the revitalizing and renewing mystery that is one's spouse require imagination, confidence, and openness of the sort that is all too rare at any time in life.

Mary, the renewing virgin mother full of grace, stands as an implacable symbol that renewal is possible, that one can begin again just as humankind did when Jesus came into the world. One can trust, one can take risks, one can begin to explore the mysterious, the numinous, which lurks just beneath the surface of the most ordinary and the most everyday, the most routine and the most matter of fact, the most commonplace. Man and woman may not want to take the image of the virgin mother of Bethlehem as a symbol to illuminate the possibility of renewal and to underpin and reinforce the efforts at renewal. They may not believe that the cosmic renewal experience at Bethlehem makes possible the transforming limit-experiences in their own relationship. If they do not wish to believe that, it is their privilege, of course. If they feel that the image of virgin mother is absurd as a symbol by which they can renew their love, then one cannot argue with them and would not try to persuade them.

They may well assert that a symbol which has stood for sexual oppression in their childhood can hardly be expected now to serve as a symbol of sexual playfulness.[9] In fact, whatever they may say, it is still the case that the virgin mother is a symbol for renewal, of beginning again, of starting all over again; it is a symbol of possibility. Mary as the protector of sexual playfulness in an ever-renewing relationship between husband and wife may be offensive to puritans and ridiculous to those who think all possibility of renewal has gone out of their relationship. Mary as the protector and proponent of renewal through sexual playfulness is consistent with the very deepest meanings of the Mary myth. Mary supports renewal, rebirth, starting all over, beginning again wherever such frightening, fascinating, wonderful experiences are to be found. Falling in love again, we are told by those who have done it, is much more fun than the first time around. Similarly, being born again was a much greater adventure for the human race than being born for the first time.

Venantius sings of the glory of the virgin mother who renews
the cosmos:

>Where troops of virgins follow the Lamb
>Through the streets of the golden city,
>Who is she walks in the lily throng
>Clothed with the sun,
>Her mantle flowing like an azure wave
>To the jewel pavement?
>High in her arms for all to adore
>She holds a Man-Child.
>She leads the mystic song that swells and soars
>Like the noise of many waters,
>With the voice of her own *Magnificat*.
>The glory of virgins is she, a maiden mother.
>O Mary, where your Jesus leads, you follow,
>The first of pearl-pure human souls.
>The prize that reckless Eve has tossed away,
>You stretch a generous hand to give again,
>And draw the earth's sad exiles
>To their promised land of joy.
>O doorway of the mighty King!
>O radiant threshold of His light!
>Life-giving Virgin!
>Nations redeemed praise you with jubilation.
>Jesus, Son of Mary,
>Father and loving Spirit,
>Glory to You forever and ever. Amen.

>"O Glory of Virgins" (*O gloriosa virginum*)
>by Venantius Fortunatus (530–609)
>(Translated from the Latin by Sister Maura)

A medieval German bard sees Mary passing through the forest
with blossoms of renewal springing up in her wake:

>Mary went through the thorn-wood wild;
>Mary went through the thorn-wood wild
>That had borne no blossom for seven years.
>
>What did she carry beneath her heart?
>Without a pang—a little child
>She carried gently beneath her heart.

And on the thorn-boughs roses stood
As she carried the sweet child through the wood;
Upon the thorn-boughs roses stood.

"Mary Passes" (Maria durch den Dornewald ging)

The strange, complex, half-mad genius Savonarola sees Mary renewing the city of Florence after the plague has passed:

O Star of Galilee,
Shining over earth's dark sea,
Shed thy glorious light on me.

Queen of clemency and love,
Be my advocate above,
And through Christ all sin remove.

When the angel called thee blest,
And with transports filled thy breast,
Thy high Lord became thy guest.

Earth's purest creature thou,
In the heavens exulting now,
With a halo round thy brow.

Beauty beams in every trace
Of the Virgin-Mother's face,
Full of glory and of grace—

A Beacon to the just,
To the sinner hope and trust,
Joy of the angel-host.

Ever-glorified, thy throne
Is where thy blessed Son
Doth reign: through Him alone,

All pestilence shall cease,
And sin and strife decrease,
And the kingdom come of peace.

"O Star of Galilee" by Girolamo Savonarola (1492–1498)
(Translated from the Latin by R. R. Madden)

Shelley, in the midst of his incorrigible love affair with nature, sees Mary lurking behind transforming dynamisms of the world and pleads with her to eliminate the imperfections of his work:

Seraph of Heaven! too gentle to be human,
Veiling beneath that radiant form of Woman
All that is insupportable in thee
Of light, and love, and immortality!
Sweet Benediction in the eternal Curse!
Veiled Glory of this lampless Universe!
Thou Moon beyond the clouds! Thou living Form
Among the Dead! Thou Star above the Storm!
Thou Wonder, and thou Beauty, and thou Terror!
Thou Harmony of Nature's art! Thou Mirror
In whom, as in the splendour of the Sun,
All shapes look glorious which thou gazest on!
Ay, even the dim words which obscure thee now
Flash, lighting-like, with unaccustomed glow;
I pray thee that thou blot from this sad song
All of its much mortality and wrong,
With those clear drops, which start like sacred dew
From the twin lights thy sweet soul darkens through,
Weeping, till sorrow becomes ecstasy:
Then smile on it, so that it may not die.

"Seraph of Heaven" (From *Epipsychidion*, lines 21–40)
by Percy Bysshe Shelley (1792–1822)

Henry Adams, having looked at the smile on the Virgin of
Chartres and having prayed ironically to the Dynamo, comes
back to the Virgin to pray "Before your majesty of grace and
love,/ The purity, the beauty and the faith;/ The depth of tenderness beneath; above,/ The glory of the life and of the death."
He prays to her now as he imagines he prayed once before with
Saint Bernard and Saint Louis:

Help me to see! not with my mimic sight—
  With yours! which carried radiance, like the sun,
Giving the rays you saw with—light in light—
  Tying all suns and stars and worlds in one.

Help me to know! not with my mocking art—
  With you, who knew yourself unbound by laws;
Gave God your strength, your life, your sight, your heart,
  And took from him the Thought that Is—the Cause.

Help me to feel! not with my insect sense,—
  With yours that felt all life alive in you;
Infinite heart beating at your expense;
  Infinite passion breathing the breath you drew!

Help me to bear! not my own baby load,
  But yours; who bore the failure of the light,
The strength, the knowledge and the thought of God,—
  The futile folly of the Infinite!

"Prayer to the Virgin of Chartres" by Henry Adams (1838–1918)

It may be Chicago chauvinism on my part, but my favorite image of the mystical transforming virgin is the El Greco *Assumption* in the Chicago Art Institute. The lovely Spanish girl with her broadly flowing red and blue robes is lifted up to renewing heaven, and at the same time she bathes in new light the whole world beneath her. And one can go back to the fifth-century praying Virgin at the archbishop's palace at Ravenna to see the outstretched arms of the virgin mother looking very much like Sophia or a Greek muse or a Cretan goddess of renewal from two millennia before. Clearly, her arms are outstretched in a plea for protection for all of us who are desperately trying to survive and renew ourselves. Roger van der Weyden's Virgin as intercessor is praying for us that we might be renewed, that we might be able to start over again. The beautiful woman being crowned by Jesus and the Father in Velasquez's *Coronation of the Virgin* represents the renewed, revivified humankind if anyone ever has. And in both El Greco's and Michelangelo's *Last Judgments* we see Mary, the tender, renewing, protecting mother, interceding for us against the stern punishments of divine justice.[10]

The virgin mother stands for a second chance. In pagan antiquity, in the depths of the human psyche, in the structures of human experience, in the renewed humankind depicted by the paintings of El Greco and Velasquez, in the passionate plea for protection from such diverse characters as Shelley and Savonarola, and in the vision of the possibility of renewal in the medieval German singer, and the tired, weary New England aristocrat, Henry Adams.

It is possible to start over again, to begin anew, to be reborn.
If only we were not so tired.

> Fair is the hue of your mantle, Mary—
>   (Take me to shelter, take me to hide!)
> *From the deep skies of Heaven it drank all its color,*
>   *In the deep pools of Heaven my mantle was dyed.*
>
> Fine is the cloth of your mantle, Mary—
>   (Take me to shelter, take me to hide!)
> *Ah, careful was the carding and careful the spinning,*
>   *And piteous the shearing of my dear Lamb's side.*
>
> Warm is the web of your mantle, Mary—
>   (Take me to shelter, take me to hide!)
> *It is woven of rare wool, woven of fair wool—*
>   *The soft white fleece of my Lamb Who died.*
>
> Draped like a queen's is your mantle, Mary—
>   (Take me to shelter, take me to hide!)
> *Yea, God hath exalted His handmaid, Who made me*
>   *Mother of His Word and His Spirit's bride.*
>
> Full are the folds of your mantle, Mary—
>   (Take me to shelter, take me to hide!)
> *That all generations be shielded and succored,*
>   *The cloak of their Mother is a deep cloak and wide.*
>
> Ah, wrap me around with your mantle, Mary—
>   (Take me to shelter, take me to hide!)
> *Child of my sword-pierced soul, I shall guard you,*
>   *Little blood-brother of the Crucified.*

"The Mantle of Mary"—Patrick O'Connor (1899–) *

VIRGO

Experience of Sexual Differentiation	Transforming, inspiring, renewing
Biological Origin	Arousal, heightened consciousness (face-eyes)

* Appeared in *I Sing of a Maiden: The Mary Book of Verse* by Sister M. Therese (New York: Macmillan, 1947), p. 320.

Cognate Symbols	Moon, lotus, lily
Ancient Goddesses	Shakti, Kwan-yin, Muse, Sophia, Tara
Type	Eve, the beginning
Mary Symbol	Virgin full of grace, the new beginning
Existential Need	Weariness
Limit-Experience	Renewal, transformation
Grace that is Given	Implacable fidelity of life-giving love, which is also life-renewing
Illumination—Restructuring of Perceptions	Trust
Action	Commitment
Man-Woman Implication	Both man and woman can inspire and renew, and can surrender to inspiration and renewal
Poem	Percy Bysshe Shelley, "Seraph of Heaven"
Plastic Art	El Greco, *The Assumption*

Part IV

SPONSA

GARDENER IN A BIKINI
(For Norman and Lou and the boys down at the harbor)

Not a full-blown classic nude
Nor an overdressed, fluffy Victorian
But Earth Mother on the American Plan
Brown, tall, supple
Womanly splendors taut and trim
Lithe nakedness made even more appealing
    by a few ounces of pale blue cloth
And tenuous bits of string.

Girlish allurements to be enjoyed
But not in passive repose
Neither statue nor bathing beauty
But Cybele in movement, most seductive
With youthful body hard at work
In the vigorous ordering of your garden.

Ethnic Venus with a swinging hoe
Each disciplined movement of arm and handle
Hip and thigh, a creamy tasty delight
Even to the angels who pause in work
    to marvel at the Creator's designing wit
And enjoy the noontime show.

Middle western nymph, cool, poised, confident
Heedlessly unaware and yet proudly aware
    of your own unclothed loveliness
Slender waist, long tan legs,
Flat belly, soft and shapely shoulders,
Curving back, caressed by a single lucky strap
A public indecency in most ages past
Now a familiar scenic attraction
On any summer day.

Engineered, machined, mass produced? Well, maybe
But the boys in the slow moving cars don't mind
As they envy the roses their start of delight
    when you swiftly bend over them
To dispatch an offending weed
And your rich full breasts
Push against thin blue restraint

Eager to spill out among the flowers
And dim the luster of their blossoms
While your rounded derriere stretches tight
The snug bikini bottom
And invites a friendly swat
From every passing male.

Elegant and delectable innocent
Sexy, bouncy and a good gardener too
Free as few women have ever been
To sport unclad in the summer sunlight
To be yourself, to reach for life
To be mistress of your own fulness
Come a long way, but expecting much more
Inviting affection, promising pleasure, demanding happiness
A big demand and requiring more from you
    than piebald breasts and saucy tail
(Though in truth they will surely help)
And much from the rest of us too.

Yet you know little of life and love
And nothing of suffering and old age
The bittersweet pleasures and the numbing pains
    that too quickly dim the youthful glow
Nor will you escape the greedy death
Which already has turned the leaves you rake
A dry and dusty brown.

But at this garden noon, I do not doubt
That the beauty from which you came
Captivated by his(her) own creation
Seduced by his(her) own seduction
Will fall victim to your active charms
And be caught in his(her) own trip of love.
Your grace will never end.

                         A.M.G.

Chapter *7*

SPONSA
AVE MARIS STELLA

The Madonna and Virgo symbols both deal with the giving of life. That which is beneath and beyond and within and outside of everything both gives life and renews it. The mother is the source of physical life, the virgin mother the source of spiritual renewal. The other two images, Sponsa and Pietà, are "death" images. The Pietà receives us in loving tenderness back into the womb of the earth at the end of life; the Sponsa, the seductress, deprives us of the individuality and the rationality of life in the frenzy of orgasmic release. Orgasm is a kind of death in that our other interests and concerns, even the other functions of our bodies, are temporarily suspended as our whole beings concentrate on the release that comes from sexual union. For a brief instant it is almost as though we have stopped living and have completely been absorbed by the elementary biological forces of the universe. With the Pietà we experience permanent death, and whether it is pleasurable or not remains to be seen.

Just as there is considerable difficulty in adjusting our perspective to understand the relevance to the contemporary world of Mary as virgin mother, so there are difficulties and obstacles that must be eliminated before we can understand Mary as a symbol of the limit-experience of sexual differentiation as manifested in sexual passion. It might be argued that Mary didn't have sexual intercourse, so how could she possibly symbolize the intercourse experience, particularly since Catholic Christianity has maintained, and apparently still maintains that it is better not to have sexual intercourse than to have it? Indeed, the church even once maintained through some of its greatest theologians that sexual intercourse was sinful even between husband and wife if it was done "merely" for pleasure.

Physical desire is the most obvious, the most demanding, the most disturbing, and the most intensely pleasurable aspect of sexual differentiation. Spiritual love, transformation, constant mutual renewal may have more long-run psychological payoff; they may also be essential for the creation of a context of relationship in which physical love may survive and develop. Nonetheless, for sheer intensity of pleasure, orgasm simply can't be beat—a phenomenon that must have been obvious to the human race from the very first time it began to reflect on anything. There is good and bad sex, of course; still, bad sex is better than no sex, and about this bit of folk wisdom there is no disagreement.

The overwhelming power and pleasure of physical union between the sexes was obviously sacred to early humankind. It was terrifying and frightening in its capacity to absorb the total concern of the individual. When its furies were released the fragile social structure of the primitive tribe or the archaic village could be torn apart. A band of hunters or warriors or shepherds returned to the camp with just one thing in mind: they wanted women. If it was their own camp, their own women would do; but if it was the camp of another tribe, their women would do too. Nothing else mattered until this primal need was satisfied. Sexuality might indeed be something sacred, because it was the source of the fertility which kept life going; but it was also sacred because of the terrifying strength of its demands, the intensity of its pleasures and the temporary destruction of the capacity to do anything else when caught in the heat of sexual arousal.[1]

Lust is the passionate desire for union with the body of a member of the opposite sex. It is, of course, fundamentally a matter of hormone levels in our bloodstreams, but since humankind is an interpreting animal, one who of necessity gives meaning to all his experiences, lust and the tension release which satisfies it are far more than biological and physiological phenomena. Because of their intense power and force, they are interpreted and given meaning within a context of sacredness.

The various fertility goddesses could easily be transformed into goddesses of orgy and orgasm. Festivals in honor of Lilith, Astarte, Aphrodite, and Venus may have begun primarily with a concern about integrating humanity into the fertility process of the universe; but the ritual intercourse frequently involved in such cults was undoubtedly pleasurable. As human religions evolved, in many cases the ritual intercourse became an end in itself. To please the goddess of fertility and to integrate oneself into the life-giving processes was distinctly a matter of secondary and often unremembered importance as the fertility cults developed—or decayed.

Once a ritual or a festival became identified with the breaking down of sexual restraints that were necessary to keep a community together, the breaking down became the important phenomenon and its ritual significance was easily forgotten. We gather on New Year's Eve to celebrate the end of an old year and the beginning of a new one; but after a while, that's hardly the name of the game. We go off to New Orleans at Mardi Gras time to prepare for Lent. Similarly, what remains of the *Carnivale* in Europe, particularly in Germany, may in principle also be a preparation for Lent—but who keeps Lent anymore?

So, too, the rites marking the change of the season—the winter and summer solstices, the vernal and autumnal equinoxes—are theoretical times when one celebrates the death and rebirth of the god of light, while at the same time commemorating the harvest, the vintage, and the eventual promise of the return of nature. As events dealing with light, fertility, and life, these four seasonal changes easily became involved with sexual differentiation, and with an understandable leap, with rituals of sexual release. The pent-up and repressed sexual energies of the society were unleashed first of all to unite oneself and one's society with the primal reproductive powers of the cosmos, but also, secondarily, to provide socially legitimate escape from sexual tensions. By the time of the Saturnalia, as we know it in the Roman Republic and Empire, the primitive and archaic religious overtones were long since lost. The Saturnalia was a feast of lust in which one worshiped (if that is the word) sexual pleasure. As a social function, it doubtless had a utility of a sort, but any connection with the old fertility rites of the mother goddess was vestigial. The immense power and pleasure of sexual release was honored, and the sexual goddesses like Venus and Aphrodite became the most important feminine deities in the pantheon. Lots of people had a rip-roaring good time.

I would not suggest that ritual orgies were without religious experience. On the contrary, the breaking down of barriers and the reversal of roles were a return to primal undifferentiation, a return to the *coincidentia oppositorum* which was supposed to mark the Beginning. There was religious and cosmological symbolism as well as the release of social tensions in a festival in which sexual limitations and restrictions were swept away. Furthermore, there was surely a valid religious insight that lust reflects a divine power in humankind; but as we moderns need little imagination to realize, it was very easy for the religious dimension of orgasmic festivals to get lost. Was Venus a goddess to be worshiped or simply a girl to be lusted after? For most people she was probably both, but in very uneven proportions.

The religious insight about the divine aspects of lust go back almost to the dawn of human religion as we know it, insofar as we know anything about it. In some religions the physical world emerged as the result of intercourse between the male and the female deity. In others, it is the lust of the divine beings for one another that produces the rebirth of spring each year, and in still others it is lust and passion between a particular people and its god—whether that god be male or female—that ensures the survival and perpetuation of the tribe. The continuation of its harvest and its vintages were in fact the result of intercourse (sometimes ritually reenacted with temple priestesses) between the deity and its people. The Israelites were not the first people to imagine that their god had embarked on a love affair with them. What was unusual about the divine romance with Israel was not the romance but the god who had fallen in love so passionately with his people.

Nor is it in principle an unreasonable assumption about the

deity that with the exception of hunger and the protection of one's life there are no human passions anywhere near as powerful as the desire for sexual release when aroused. The sweating, writhing, screaming frenzy of a man and woman in the final stages of intercourse is evidence of how fierce and furious is sexual desire. Something that strong, humankind has argued traditionally, must give us some hints about whatever is ultimate, absolute, and final. If lust is powerful and God is powerful, then there may well be some kind of lust in God, or some thing in God which is as powerful in him as lust is in us. But what could be the object of divine lust? It might be other dieties, or it might be individual human maidens with whom the god becomes enamored, or it might be the whole of his creation, particularly his people. Lust is the desire for unity, the desire to merge one's personality, however transiently, with another's, to lose oneself in the breaking down of the barrier of sexual differentiation, to form a oneness out of two fleshes. If God craved unity the way we crave the body of another, then who was the object of his craving for unity? The answer was a startling, and it must have seemed blasphemous to many, insight: God craved union with us. Once people began to think that way, a decisive revolution had occurred in human religious consciousness. It might be a long time before the kind of God who had fallen in love with his creatures would be the sort of person you would invite to your house for supper. After all, many of those lusty, roustabout, horny gods of antiquity were thoroughly disreputable characters. Yahweh, as in other things, was something else altogether. It was not the bodies of your maidens or your matrons He wanted; it was the whole personality, body and soul, of the people. As time went on, it became clear that he wanted the whole personality, body and soul, of each individual of the people. Yahweh lusted not after our bodies but after us, and then, religiously speaking, it became a whole new game.

So the people became the bride of Yahweh, and Israel, God's people, became personified as the Daughter of Zion for whom Yahweh felt a passionate lust, a lust which would produce eventually a messiah, who in his turn would preside over Yahweh's messianic age. We may have come a long way from orgies at the temple of Venus to Yahweh's passion for the Daughter of Zion. The religious thought has been transformed obviously, refined and elevated; but the imagery and the religious insight are fundamentally the same: in God's relationship to us, there is something like the passionate longing that we feel at the height of our lust for the body of one who is sexually different from us. God may be the passionate aggressive male pursuing us in a frenzy of sexual arousal (and such images are frequent enough in the later prophets of the Old Testament), or he may be a woman tempting us, teasing us, leading us on alternately discouraging and encouraging us, promising, revealing, hiding, disclosing, covering, uncovering, but always enticing us. Whether God is the passionate aggressor or the passionate temptress, the message is the same: God wants us and he is leading us on or pursuing us toward eventual union.

In the Old Testament the image of the Daughter of Zion is the corporate personality, Israel, which is the object of Yahweh's passionate love. In the New Testament and later Mariology it is Mary who is the individual person for whom God felt a passionate attraction. This merely conveys the age-old human insight that God loves us with a power and force and strength that makes human sexual arousal look mild and moderate by comparison. A man pursuing the body of a woman who has utterly enthralled him (captivated, imprisoned, captured—whatever other similar word of enslavement might be appropriate) so that nothing will stand in his way or stop him until he has merged his body with hers is a weak and meek thing compared to the way the absolute feels about us. A woman who uses every guile and wile and attractiveness, every inch of her flesh, every curve of her body to capture a man she passionately wants looks modest when compared with the wanton deity who has created the entire glorious universe to attract and seduce us.

This religious insight may be offensive to some and absurd to others, but it is what Mary, the Daughter of Zion, with whom Yahweh has fallen in love, represents. We may reject as ridiculous the notion that God feels about us the way we do about a man or a woman in the height of sexual arousal. Things *cannot* be that way; it would either be offensive or ludicrous. For some, the image of a sexually aroused God is dirty, for others, it is altogether too good to be true, and we know better than to believe it. However, such an image is still one of the fundamental themes of the Yahwistic religion, and it is captured for Christianity by the symbol of Mary, Daughter of Zion.

The symbols can be played in two directions. We can think of God as a sexual attacker aggressively pursuing us, or we can think of God as the sensual temptress seductively attracting us. Once one concedes the androgyny of God, either approach is valid; or, more properly, both approaches are valid. Indeed such is the case in many human love affairs where the pursuer is pursued. The sexually attacking male, if he has any skills at all, is teasing, arousing, enticing; and the sexually tempting female, if she has any wiles at all, knows when to stop being passive and take the offensive. Our religious insight as Christians leads us to believe that God, too, plays the game both ways.

If there is a God, it is surely the case that he both seduces and attacks us, both tempts us and pursues us. We may be horrified to think of him in such a way either because we think that such a God is inappropriate, or (and more correctly it seems to me) because such a God is too frightening. Of course there is no obligation to think of God that way. One can conceptualize the deity in any way one wants. The point is that if one concedes there is a God involved in the human condition, the image of temptation and pursuit becomes inevitable. If you don't like the image, don't use it, but to deny its validity and inevitability you have got to deny either the existence of passionate love at the core of the universe or assert that there is such a passionate love but that for some inexplicable reason it doesn't care much about us.

So Mary is the spouse of Yahweh, the one after whom Yahweh lusts. But each of us is the spouse of Yahweh, and whether we want to think of God as feminine or masculine, as attacking us or tempting us, is entirely a matter of our own personal religious choice and taste. God as the pursuing male is an image that is open and explicit in the Christian religion; but God as the woman, attractive, charming, fascinating, is also strongly pictured in the Christian heritage through the Mary myth. Mary reveals God to us as alluring, tempting, charming, arousing, attracting.

The existential need as a prelude to the limit-experience of an encounter with a passionately aroused Being is, I think, a combination of alienation, constriction, restraint, loneliness. We are cut off; we are alone; we are isolated; we are alienated; we are hemmed in, restricted, hung up, constrained by our own fears, anxieties, suspicions, skepticism, cynicism. We then encounter a thing which invades our personality, attracts our attention, demands our interest, arouses our wonder and awe, and consumes us with its "being-ness." The thing, whatever it is, becomes a symbol for us, a sacrament, a revelation of gifted-ness precisely insofar as it can momentarily command our whole attention, attract our whole selfhood, and impose upon us the obligation to abandon ourselves to it completely. That thing-turned-symbol under the influence of Mary as Sponsa can be almost anything. Most obviously it will be a member of the opposite sex, but even the grass growing on the dune can invade me, take me over, absorb my attention, and demand that for a few moments at least, I became abandoned to it, totally absorbed by the wonder and marvel of its being, possessed by its attractiveness, entranced by its graciousness, dominated by the goodness for which it is a sacrament.

In the act of abandoning myself through the gift of the thing-turned-symbol, I abandon my old structures of perception. They are shattered. It is no longer necessary to be restrained, constricted, cut off, suspicious. Having given myself over to this being, I can, if I will, give myself over to Being. The new structures of perception which emerge from the limit-experience are looser, more open, more flexible, more sensitive, more in communion with other things. I now approach the world not with fear, suspicion, or inhibition but with joy, liberation, abandonment.

In lovemaking there comes a point when abandonment of some sort takes over. The proprieties, the decencies, the restraints drop away and basic, elemental urges dominate. When that point of abandonment is reached, both partners know that they will couple. There is nothing tentative, preliminary, or preparatory left. The situation is to a considerable extent, though not completely, of course, dominated by the biology and physiology of their bodies. They have "let go"; they have "turned on"; they have yielded themselves more or less willingly, more or less skillfully, more or less gracefully, more or less pleasurably to one another. The surge of liberation, of abandonment, of letting go in intercourse is paradigmatic of the letting go which happens in the limit-experience.[2]

When abandonment of any sort becomes a limit-experience, a sacrament of grace, a revelation, through the impact on us of the being of the thing to which we have given ourself, then there is revealed to us the glorious gift and liberating seductiveness and passion of the ultimate. In the limit-experience of abandoning ourself, we encounter the other, which has both attracted and pursued us into this act of abandonment. We have met only life-giving love, not only life-renewing love but now also pursuing and attracting love, challenging and demanding love, love which wishes to absorb us, love which invites us to lose our self in it, love which demands abandonment and which repays our abandonment with freedom.

Freedom is the illumination offered to us through our restructured perceptions when we permit ourselves to fall under the spell of Mary, Daughter of Zion, the beloved Sponsa of Yahweh. If the world is animated by a passionate lover, the cosmos is directed by a seductive temptress; if our life is dominated and guided by one who is calling us to ever greater love, then there is nothing to be afraid of. Oh, we still have our fears, our existential fear of nothingness, our fear of death, our inhibitions. Our neurotic little fears that we so carefully preserve from childhood are real enough, but they do not cut us off from others, they do not imprison us, they do not bog us down, they do not constrict or restrain us. We have abandoned ourselves to a goodness that we have encountered and experienced, to a grace that has taken possession of us; and we are free to live and love and laugh and rejoice.

So much of our life is constraint. We are afraid of what others will say, afraid of what will happen. We are afraid of losing the few things we have acquired. We fear having our defenses swept away, of being stripped naked psychologically to stand revealed as utterly worthless, a "no thing." If we give ourselves over to joy and freedom, all these precious things we have will be lost, and from being a "no thing" we will slip into nonbeing; we will merely die, we will cease to exist.

Mary, the Daughter of Zion, Mary, the beloved Sponsa of God, Mary, the Bride of Yahweh, stands as a symbol that exactly the opposite possibility is available to us. If we merely abandon ourselves to the passionate goodness in the universe, if we say with her, "Be it done unto me according to Thy word," then we become free. (This is, incidentally, a long process, not a single decision. It may require and can coexist with a therapeutic experience.)

If you are imprisoned in the chains of your own fear, then there is nothing to celebrate, but if you are liberated by a love that captivates your heart, then not only can you celebrate, you must celebrate. Mary the Madonna moves us to the action of protecting and enriching the world, Mary the Virgin moves us to the sustained commitment to the people of the world, and Mary the Sponsa moves us to joyous celebration of the glories of the world. It is of the nature of the symbol, as we observed in Chapter 2, that it moves us first to action and then to reflection. Our theologizing about the salvation revealed in the Daughter of Zion is not a precondition to our celebration. On the contrary, our lives of celebration are the phenomenon with which theology begins to reflect. Joy is a *locus theologicus,* an occasion for theologizing and not the result of it. In Luke's infancy narratives, Mary sings a hymn of praise; she does not write a doctoral dissertation or an article for a scholarly journal.

I spoke in an earlier chapter of the exuberance of the early Christians which permitted them to absorb so many of the good things they beheld in paganism and make them their own. The exuberance that resulted from their encounter with God proved hard to sustain. Some Christians still have it, of course, but to all too many Christians, Teresa of Avila's prayer that God "deliver us from sour-faced saints" still applies. Too many of us have lost our energy and our enthusiasm, our faith in the power of rationality, civility, liberal democracy, and scientific technology to humanize the planet. I am in categoric disagreement with the prophets of doom and the mad, self-destructive proponents of zero economic growth. I do not accept an economic or scientific analysis which views either natural resources or energy as vanishing from the planet. On the contrary, I think the evidence suggests just the opposite. There is reason for short-term concern, of course, about the expanding populations of certain countries of the world and the short-run supply of energy, particularly as long as the rulers of the oil-producing countries can casually threaten to demolish the world's economy. I certainly do not see any reason for us to be wasteful of resources either. There are problems of both environment and resources. There will likely be famine in the short run no matter how generous the developed countries are, there may be serious worldwide economic depression within a decade or so, and we could blunder into ecodisasters (though probably not anything like the ecodisaster of the Black Death). But over the long run there seems to be no solid economic reason to abandon faith in science, technology, civility, or the liberal democratic system. Indeed, as I read Robert Heilbroner, his problems are not ultimately political, social, or economic. He has lost his faith in human nature and human society.

My call for joy and celebration is not based on naïvete about the economic, environmental, and population problems of the world. Such problems are far more serious than many American Catholic Christians are willing to admit to themselves; they are not nearly as disastrous as some of the prophets of doom would claim. In the final analysis, however, Christian joy and celebration cannot be rooted in economic analysis. We rejoice in having abandoned ourselves in passionate love of an aggressive and seductive deity regardless of the economic and political outlook. We can chant the Magnificat to the Daughter of Zion even with the Black Death moving through the streets of our city.

If we as American Catholics think it is necessary to be gloomy to gain acceptance in some quarters—to be invited to Martha's Vineyard for a summer weekend among the disenchanted intellectual and cultural elites, for example—then by all means let us be gloomy, but let us also at least admit to ourselves that it's a game we are playing. We don't really mean it. Let us retreat into caves or catacombs at night, gather around the statue of the virgin and laugh and stamp our feet in joy. We fooled the prophets of doom once again. Let us never take the prophets of doom seriously, and heaven save us from taking ourselves seriously. Let us stand in the shadow of Mary, with her gentle, half-amused smile, and abandon ourselves to the exuberance and joy which comes from being Christian.

All this may not be your cup of tea. You may not enjoy abandoning yourself to celebration and exuberance. You may think there are too many things wrong with the world and with the human race to permit any expression less than sour to pass over your face. I shall not attempt to persuade you, but we shall miss you among Mary's company. You have misunderstood altogether what God revealed to us in his love for the Daughter of Zion.

Finally, if there is passion in the universe, indeed unrestrained passion which is both reflected in and the cause of human passion, then the passions we humans feel for one another have certainly been legitimated, reinforced, sanctified. If we are to abandon ourselves in joyous celebration to passionate being, then surely it is not only legitimate but virtuous to abandon ourselves in joyous celebration to one another. Granting that social conventions must necessarily restrain the raw, elemental power of sexual arousal from tearing society apart, and granting, too, that there will be differences of opinion and swings of fashion back and forth between restraint and liberty in the expression of social conventions, there are still no grounds in the Mary myth for prudery, puritanism, inhibition, frigidity in the relationship between husband and wife. On the contrary, the Mary myth incarnates the worldview which advocates joyous abandonment of restraint in the relationship between a man and woman who are committed to one another. Discretion, respect for privacy, good taste, sensitivity are all still required; but experimentation, playfulness, joyous abandonment ought to be characteristic of the sexual relationship of those who believe that God is a passionate lover, a ravisher, a seducer, a temptress all combined.

It is not always the case, and it has not always been the case. One need only read many of the great Christian theologians like St. Augustine to see that a Platonic suspicion of human sexuality has pervaded Christian thinking for a long, long time. One need only recall the mission sermons of not so long ago to see that grass roots Christianity was pervaded by the worst kind of prudery and puritanism. There are no grounds for either Platonism or puritanism in the Christian symbol system and no grounds for it in the myth of Mary the Daughter of Zion after whom Yahweh lusted (if, in the New Testament, only as a corporate personality).

That both Platonism and puritanism survived as long as they did is merely evidence of how long it takes a new mythology, a new set of symbols to break the hold of an old worldview. The history of sexual thought in the Christian era has yet to be written. Most scholars who address themselves to it do so with little data and lots of preconceived notions. One of the few who have approached the matter with both an open mind and a respect for data is Herbert Richardson in his book *Nun, Witch and Playmate.*[3] Richardson argues that the emphasis on virginity in the Christian tradition was in fact a reaction against Platonic views of sexuality in the world of Hellenistic antiquity into which Christianity came. The human spirit was viewed as a slave, or at least a prisoner, of the physical body, particularly of its sexuality. Differentiation between the sexes was absolute, and the woman was absolutely inferior because she was more captive of her sex than the man and more likely to imprison him in the demands of her body. "Real" friendship was spiritual and only possible between members of one's own sex. One had a wife, of course, for release of sexual tension and so that the family might be perpetuated, but friendship was another matter. Often, of course, there were sexual overtones to the friendship, though Plato argued through Socrates that ideal friendship was independent of the body.

In Richardson's view of things, the Christian attitude was quite different. Sexual differentiation could be transcended, and men and women could be friends in the power of the Lord Jesus. It might be necessary for them both to be virginal in order to sustain such a friendship, but virginity was then seen, not as a judgment that sexuality was evil but an act of faith that in Jesus friendship was no longer constrained by sexual differentiation. It was out of this perspective, Richardson argues, that the courtly romantic love of the Middle Ages first emerged, with its emphasis on erotic but not genital sexuality; and then, in more recent times, the revolutionary notion that marriages and friendship could be combined. According to Richardson, virginity as a way of life was a step in an historical evolutionary process toward our present day notion of the combination of marriage, romantic sex, and friendship—an ideal toward which most humans are still striving.

There is a certain plausibility in his theory; it seems to fit the data currently available to us. But we should not forget another source of Christian faith and practice, besides the Platonism of the high theological tradition and the puritanism of some of the expressions of practical moral guidance, as Father Godfrey Dieckman has repeatedly insisted. If one looks at the liturgy, particularly the worship service around the celebration of marriage, one finds an entirely different set of themes. Marriage was a sacrament, a revelatory event. It disclosed the love of God for his people, the church. There was no trace of puritanism, prudery, Platonism there. To the extent that there were any influences outside the Christian symbol system, they were from the relatively joyous paganism of the Teutonic and Celtic tribes, and not of the grim and glum paganism of the neo-Platonic empire. The mixture of old fertility and sexual practices with the new Christian symbols of God's love for his people and of the church as the bride of Christ may have been uneven and uneasy, but apparently it never bothered the people themselves very much. There is still much research to do on this subject, and as far as I am aware, not many people are doing it. An interesting folk custom of peasant Poland is that the bride and groom recited the Magnificat after their first union. I am dazzled by the rich religious and sexual implications of such a custom. Doubtless, pagan fertility goddesses and goddesses of sexual love lurked around the marriage bed in pre-Christian times, but in this peasant custom, the Slavic versions of Aphrodite and Juno are dispatched by the Daughter of Zion, whose words are spoken by the bridal couple as they rejoice and give thanks to God over the union they have begun. There is no Platonism, no puritanism, and no paganism either in such a custom. In terms of the religious symbolism of the Mary myth, such a custom was profoundly right.

What of celibacy, then? What of those who choose to forgo orgasmic satisfaction and human love in marital intimacy? Richardson sees it as a step in the evolution of Christian thinking. Most Protestant Christians and an increasing number of Catholic Christians (perhaps even a majority) are now convinced that consecrated virginity is outmoded, that happiness, self-fulfillment, good physical and mental health require that one have a spouse. Some would even suggest that those who chose celibacy in the past were probably a bit strange, and those who choose it today, in a post-Freudian age, are crazy. Does my suggestion that Mary, the Daughter of Zion, the beloved of Yahweh, the revelation of God's passionate lust for his creatures, a symbol which can easily preside over joyous and celebratory abandonment in marital intimacy, conflict with the existence of consecrated virginity? Does everyone, in other words, have to have orgasm? Does everyone need the warmth and intimacy of family life for their healthy physical and psychological development?

The answer is an obvious no, I think (though both the "obvious" and the "no" will be unacceptable to many readers, I fear). To write off the great celibate saints of the past as psychic misfits is a narrow, rigid intolerance of the various modalities of being-in-the-world. There is no reason in psychoanalytic theory to deny that sublimation can be psychologically healthy. Nor is there any evidence in the psychological measurement literature to show that those who lead lives of consecrated virginity are any less mature, any less fulfilled, or any less satisfied than married people. There are, God knows, misfits in the religious and priestly life, and there are certainly misfits in the married life. I doubt that their particular states of life have much to do with the dynamics of their difficulties.

Consecrated virginity is one way of responding to Yahweh's love. It is a way of reacting to the grace that is revealed to us in limit-experiences. It is a way of serving and loving other human beings. To deny that many healthy, heterosexual human beings can have rich and rewarding lives in this form of love and service is to deny an obvious fact. Because many who chose a celibate life mistakenly and are unhappy in it does not mean that by its very nature such a life need be any less happy than one of marital intimacy. Both have their problems, both have their payoffs. I very much doubt, for example, that Catholicism could have sustained the faith and the organizational commitment of the immigrants in the United States without a celibate clergy and religious. Furthermore, to deny that a life of such service is a mystery, a sign, a revelatory act, a grace which reveals to others the presence of a passionately loving God—or at least the conviction of human being that there is such a passionately loving God—is to deny the obvious.

The charism of a vocation of consecrated virginity is not given to everyone. Part of the problem today may be that not so long ago we imposed such charisms on people who didn't have them. Such a style of life clearly has to be a matter of free choice. But, I will insist, there is no contradiction between such a free choice and the myth of Mary as Sponsa, the reflection of Yahweh's lust for his people. For if Mary, as that symbol, provides legitimation and reinforcement for the abandonment and the joy of orgasmic union which celebrates human life, it by no means imposes an obligation for such union. There are many ways one can abandon oneself; there are many ways to celebrate; there are many forms of service in which one can rejoice. In the Father's kingdom there are many mansions. Those who would herd everyone into just one have no respect for the variety, the diversity, the pluralism the Father encourages in his kingdom on earth.

Those Christians who would exclude consecrated virginity from an honored place in the Christian life are guilty of more than just doing violence to an ancient tradition. For what they are doing in effect is to impose an obligation to marry. It is a rigid and authoritarian dictum that one who does not marry is either a misfit, unfulfilled, or perhaps not altogether heterosexual. Such a cynical, narrow view is all too widespread in contemporary American Catholicism. This may be in part because consecrated virginity was extolled in such a way in times gone past that marriage looked decidedly second rate. Now that we celebrate the joys and glories of marital intimacy and sexual orgasm with religious support, it seems logical enough to downgrade the worth of consecrated virginity. Human beings feel it easier to say "either/or" instead of "both/and." Still, there is no reason why both states should not be glorified. Anyone who has a tolerant, open personality should find it rather easy to do so. The symbol of Mary, the virgin Daughter of Zion, is sufficiently broad to reinforce all deep, passionate, powerful commitments that we humans can make, as well as every joyous, celebratory abandonment in which we give ourselves over to the goodness of being.

Images of Mary as the beloved of a passionate God abound in the poetic literature. Thus St. John of the Cross makes clear in one of his poems the passion involved in God's choice:

Then He summoned an archangel,
Blessed Gabriel by name.
To a lowly girl called Mary
The Divine archangel came.

For with her co-operation
This great mystery could be.
With her flesh the Word was clothed
By the Blessed Trinity.

All three Persons worked that wonder,
Though in One alone 'twas done.
In the womb of Blessed Mary
Took her flesh the Incarnate Son.

He that erst had had but Father
Had a Mother likewise then,
And He was conceived in Mary,
As have been no other men.

Hers His flesh and hers His dwelling
Ere His human life began,
Wherefore He is called together
Son of God and Son of Man

"Romance VIII" by Saint John of the Cross (1542–1591)
(Translated from the Spanish by E. Allison Peers)

And Robert Southwell, who was scarcely a saint, engaged in a pun to make the same point:

Spell Eva back and Ave shall you find,
   The first began, the last reversed our harms;
An angel's witching words did Eva blind,
   And angels' Ave disenchants the charms;
Death first by woman's weakness entered in,
In woman's virtue life doth now begin.

O virgin breast! The heavens to thee incline,
   In thee their joy and sovereign they agonize;
Too mean their glory is to match with thyne,
   Whose chaste receite God more than heaven did prize.
Hail fairest heaven, that heaven and earth doth bliss,
Where virtue stars, God, Son of justice is!

With haughty mind to Godhead man aspired,
   And was by pride from the place of pleasure chased;
With loving mind our manhood God desired,
   And us by love in greater pleasure placed:
Man laboring to ascend procured our fall,
God yielding to descend cut off our thrall.

"Our Lady's Salutation" by Robert Southwell (1561–1595)

The love affair between God and Mary is celebrated in our own time by W. H. Auden in a conversation between Mary and God with Gabriel as go between:

Gabriel

Mary, in a dream of love
Playing as all children play,
For unsuspecting children may
Express in comic make-believe
The wish that later they will know
Is tragic and impossible;
Hear, child, what I am sent to tell:
Love wills your dream to happen, so
Love's will on earth may be, through you,
No longer a pretend but true.

Mary

What dancing joy would whirl
My ignorance away?

Light blazes out of the stone,
The taciturn water
Burst into music,
And warm wings throb within
The motionless rose:
What sudden rush of Power
Commands me to command?

Gabriel

When Eve, in love with her own will,
Denied the will of Love and fell,
She turned the flesh Love knew so well
To knowledge of her love until
Both love and knowledge were of sin:
What her negation wounded, may
Your affirmation heal today;
Love's will requires your own, that in
The flesh whose love you do not know,
Love's knowledge into flesh may grow.

Mary

My flesh in terror and fire
Rejoices that the Word
Who utters the world out of nothing,
As a pledge of His word to love her
Against her will, and to turn
Her desperate longing to love,
Should ask to wear me,
From now to their wedding day,
For an engagement ring.

Gabriel

Since Adam, being free to choose,
Chose to imagine he was free
To choose his own necessity,
Lost in his freedom, Man pursues
The shadow of his images:
Today the Unknown seeks the known;
What I am willed to ask, your own

Will has to answer; child, it lies
Within your power of choosing to
Conceive the Child who chooses you.*

"Dialogue between Mary and Gabriel"
(From *For the Time Being—A Christmas Oratorio*) by W. H. Auden
(1907–1974)

The haunted, melancholy Oscar Wilde looked for something else but found in Mary, the Daughter of Zion, the supreme mystery of love:

Was this His coming! I had hoped to see
A scene of wondrous glory, as was told
Of some great God who in a rain of gold
Broke open bars and fell on Danae:
Or a dread vision as when Semele,
Sickening for love and unappeased desire,
Prayed to see God's clear body, and the fire
Caught her brown limbs and slew her utterly.
With such glad dreams I sought this holy place,
And now with wondering eyes and heart I stand
Before this supreme mystery of Love:
Some kneeling girl with passionless pale face,
An angel with a lily in his hand,
And over both the white wings of a Dove.

"Ave Maria, Gratia Plena" by Oscar Wilde (1856–1900)

Francesco Petrarch, that worldly wise son of the Renaissance, felt the same throb of cosmic passion:

Fair Virgin,
   Vestured with the sun!
Bright shining one,
   Star-crowned:
Who such sweet ultimate favor found
   From all eternity
With the great primal Sun
   That from the height

* Copyright 1944 and renewed 1972 by W. H. Auden. Reprinted from *Collected Longer Poems*, by W. H. Auden, by permission of Random House, Inc. and Faber and Faber Ltd.

He stooped in thee to hide the light
  Of His Divinity:
Now shall my love upraise
New measures in thy praise,
Though to begin without thy aid were vain
  And without His,
Who, joined with thee in love, shall ever reign.
  Thee I invoke who never turned deaf ear
When ardent faith called to thee without fear.
  Virgin, if our poor misery,
    Our trafficking with pain,
In thy deep heart stir pity,
    Incline to me again;
Once more on thy sure succour now I lean,
Though of base clay am I
    And thou be Heaven's queen.

"Ode to the Virgin" by Francesco Petrarch (1304–1374) First stanza.
(Translated from the Italian by Helen Lee Peabody)

In all of these poems, there are two cross-cutting themes of passion. There is first of all the abandonment of God who gives himself over in love to his people as personified and represented by "some kneeling girl with a passionless, pale face," as Oscar Wilde puts it. There is also the theme of abandonment, of joy, of celebration, of exuberance, of freedom that comes from the poet himself, caught up as he is by the sacrament of grace, by the manifestation of gracefulness that he beholds in the virgin Daughter of Zion. Petrarch, Wilde, Auden, Southwell, John of the Cross are all very different men, but all sing in praise and exultation of what they beheld.

Paintings of the visit of the angel to Mary often portray her with such restraint that many moderns would see her as passionless. My own incorrigibly romantic tastes will be revealed no doubt with my selection of El Greco's and Fra Angelico's Annunciation paintings. The young woman of Fra Angelico seems overwhelmed, reduced to stunned silence which does not hide the passionate determination of her response. El Greco's virgin is astonished—so much so that her lovely lips are open in surprise; but she too is no weak, diffident child. Indeed, I have the impression that the virgin of El Greco's *Annunciation* can hardly wait to begin the journey to Elizabeth. She is filled with good news; she is ecstatic with joy. Her abandonment, her surrender has been an experience of wonder but also one that demands celebration.

Van der Weyden, Memling, Botticelli, and Bonfigli have all created portraits of the Daughter of Zion which are admirable in their expression of modesty, discretion, and surrender. Only Botticelli's *Daughter of Zion* (in the Uffizi), however, seems to be a woman of strength and passion, a woman capable of responding to God's strong love with a powerful love of her own. The Botticelli virgin matches God's passion with passion of her own, God's strength with strength of her own. The mere tilt of her head is proper enough, but I suspect that the propriety conceals an abandonment and joy that is both intense and utterly unshakable.

Bonfigli's adolescent in his annunciation painting has not yet responded to the message of the angel disguised as a dove, but it is quite possible that when she does, she will turn into a hoyden, running out of the house and down the road in breathless excitement. At least that's what I hope she would do.

There is a certain quietness in both the poems and the paintings of the Annunciation. Yahweh consummates his union with the Sponsa, the Daughter of Zion, subtly, gently, almost imperceptibly. It is a strange kind of passion to us humans. The passion we know is rather the opposite, so we are tempted to say that if that is how God's lust works, it must not be very powerful after all; if that is how God's hunger for union with humankind manifests itself, he can't be all that hungry. Yet even in our own experience as creatures, great passion can be communicated with the light touch of hand on hand. Moreover, and more importantly, God's ways need not be our ways. The universe apparently came into existence as the result of a shattering explosion—the proverbial "big bang" of astrophysics. How appropriate, then, for God to begin again, to renew his romance by something rather like a very light tapping on the door, so light that at first we barely hear it.

John Donne sees Yahweh's passion for Mary existing even before time began. His language is gentle, subtle, delicate, and elegant, yet fully expressive of Mary's grace.

> Salvation to all that will is nigh:
>   That All which always is All everywhere;
>   Which cannot sin, and yet, all sins must bear;
> Which cannot die, yet, cannot choose but die—
> Lo, faithful Virgin, yields himself to lie
>   In prison in thy womb; and though he there
>   Can take no sin, nor thou give, yet, he'll wear
> Taken from thence, flesh, which death's force may try.
> Ere, by the spheres time was created, thou
>   Wast in his mind—which is thy Son and Brother,
>   Whom thou conceivest—conceived; year, thou art now
> Thy Maker's Maker, and the Father's Mother:
> Thou hast Light in dark, and shut in little room
> Immensity, cloistered in thy dear womb.

"Annunciation" by John Donne (1573–1631)

SPONSA

Experience of Sexual Differentiation	Pleasure, lust
Biological Origin	Orgasm (Vulva)
Cognate Symbols	Moon, planets (Venus)
Ancient Goddesses	Venus, Astarte, Aphrodite
Type	Daughter of Zion
Mary Symbol	Sponsa, desired of Yahweh (corporate personality in the New Testament)
Existential Need	Aloneness, isolation, restriction, inhibition
Limit-Experience	Passionate abandon
Grace that is Given	A love that pursues and attracts, invades and tempts
Illumination—Restructuring of Perceptions	Freedom
Action	Celebration

Man-Woman Implication	Playful pleasure
Poem	W. H. Auden's "Dialogue between Mary and Gabriel"
Plastic Art	Botticelli's *Annunciation*

Part V

PIETÀ

THE BLACK-EYED WIFE

A great man lies dying
Gray, haggard, hollow
But there is worse than death in this room
With its thick rugs and rich drapery
Energies and forces fill the air
Fearsome, primal, ancient
Spirits, good and evil,
And something terrible in between.

I like it not
This roar of heaven's wars
My holy oils irrelevant
My priestly words drowned out
By the din of spirit's battle.

Outside the peaceful lake, the routine traffic
But here a struggle which was old when the galaxy was new.
In the next room friends' quiet conversation
Here the sizzling electricity of good and evil
Love and hate, order and chaos invisible.
Evil has come to conquer a good man's soul
Chaos to reassert its fearsome hold
Hatred to open its dread abyss.

None of this for your local parish priest
Against them my poor prayers weak and vain
I do not deal with demons and seraphim
With psychic principalities and powers
I only minister the Final Rites.

Through the demons which haunt this room
The black-eyed girl moves
With steady confidence
She knows these demons, understands their power
Young in years but as old as they
A psychic lightening rod
More a target perhaps than he.

It is for two souls they fight
Amidst the swirling currents of dark and light.
And, powers of good, as always in retreat
I'm sorry but please don't count on me.

The black-eyed wife straightens the sheet,
Smooths the spread
Gently wipes his brow
Calmly takes his hand
Softly repeats the prayers
Her sensuous warmth routs the haunting chill
The angels begin to hum
And mother church quietly goes to work.

The two mothers, church and wife,
Will not give up their son
Save to the One Who Is to Come
Then tenderly the black-eyed girl
Yields her man to another
Who some day must explain . . .

It is finished, the day is done
The demons cackle but they know they're lost
The powers crackle but their energies are spent
Strange things yet to happen
But no matter for the black-eyed woman
She weeps but she knows that she has won.

Outside the lake still serene in the setting sun
Mine a minor rule in this eery drama
And I do not want another.
Irrelevant to the mighty contenders,
Priests with holy oil are common
Indistinguishable, they come and go.
Yet Something tells me as I leave
"This night there was more at stake
Than you will ever know"
And it's nice to think
As you drive off in the night
That the side you were on
Was the side that won.

A.M.G.

Chapter 8

PIETÀ
FELIX COELI PORTA

The Pietà symbol in the Mary myth is the most complicated of the four symbols both because it combines seemingly opposite experiences and because, as Neumann suggests, the "negative elementary character" of the experience of the feminine "originates in inner experience" and cannot be derived from any "actual and evident attributes of woman." [1] Neumann asserts that the "Terrible Female" is a symbol for the unconscious, and hence the "Terrible Mother takes the form of monsters. . . ." [2] He goes on, "In the myths and tales of all peoples, ages, and countries—even in the nightmares of our own nights—witches and vampires, ghouls and specters, assail us, all terrifyingly alike." [3]

> Just as world, life, nature, and soul have been experienced as a generative and nourishing, protecting and warming Femininity, so their opposites are also perceived in the image of the Feminine; death and destruction, danger and distress, hunger and nakedness, appear as helplessness in the presence of Death and Terrible Mother.[4]

It is from the earth that life comes; it is the earth to which life returns. The earth is the great womb; it produces us in life, it devours us in death. It is the place from whence we come, the place to which we go to rot. If woman is like the womb and like the earth, then she is both the giver and the destroyer of life.

One may not have to go to the unconscious, however, to discover human experiences that may explain the relationship between the female goddess and death in most of the world's religions. Sexual intercourse, as we noted previously, is like death
in that most of our other interests and faculties are suspended
transiently, and temporarily we "lose consciousness" (if we do
not become "unconscious") at the height of pleasure. Similarly,
given the very high infant mortality rates of primitive and archaic people, the mother must have had many dead children in
her arms in the course of her childbearing years. Birth and death
were linked not only psychologically, but when home and hearth
were being assaulted, women became fully as destructive warriors as their men. Finally, when an injured shepherd or hunts-
man lay dying by the fireside, it was the woman who cradled his
head in her arms—often the same woman who brought him into
the world.

The primitive mother goddess, the goddess of earth in which
all things decay, the devourer of the dead bodies of mankind, the
mistress and the lady of the tombs, is a very ancient divine personage. In the most ancient figurines we have from India, Kali,
the goddess of death, is already the major figure in the pantheon.
Neumann describes this worthy lady in three of her manifestations:

> The most terrible of the three images of Kali is not the one
> with the inhuman many arms, hideously squatting amid a
> halo of flames, devouring the entrails that form a deathly
> umbilical cord between the corpse's open belly and her own
> gullet. Nor is it the one that, clad in the nocturnal black of
> the earth goddesses and adorned with the hacked-off hands
> and heads of her victims, stands on the corpse of Chiva—a
> barbaric specter whose exaggeration of horror makes her al-
> most unreal. The third figure seems far more frightful be-
> cause it is quieter and less barbarous. Here the hands strike
> us as human. One is extended, the other strokes the heads of
> the cobras almost as tenderly as Isis caressing the head of her
> child; and though the phallic animal breasts are repellent,
> they recall the similar breasts of the African mother goddess.
> But with its hooded head, the cobra that is twined round her

> waist like a girdle suggests the womb—here in its deadly
> aspect. This is the snake that lies coiled in the lap of the Cre-
> tan snake goddess, forms the snake robe of the Mexican
> goddess Coatlicue, and girds the loins of the Greek Gorgons.
> And the hideous bloody tiger's tongue of the goddess is the
> same as hangs down flame-sprewing between the tusks and
> bestial striped breasts of the Rangda witch, or darts from be-
> tween the gnashing fangs of the Gorgons.[5]

Hathor, the Syrian cow goddess, is a first cousin or perhaps even a sister to the hippopotamus goddess of the underworld; and Medusa, the Gorgon, and Hecate are similar forms of the feminine as destructive death. However, if one really wants to encounter the Terrible Mother in all her unbridled fury, one must go to Mexico. Ilamatecuhtli, the Aztec goddess of death, presides over human sacrifices and destroys her son, the male warrior god, after ripping out his heart and castrating him. She must be one of the most degraded religious conceptions humankind has yet produced.

Neumann points out that some of the death goddesses are al-most the mother goddesses in slightly different forms. Demeter, Ishtar, and Hathor are normally life-producing goddesses, but they can also be life-destroying goddesses. They are keepers of the gate of life and can make life stand still by closing the womb of living creatures. They may be mistresses of the East Gate, the Gate of Life, and at the same time preside over the West Gate, the Gate of Death and Hell. (The word "hell" is derived from the German goddess of the underworld, "Helle.")

This ambivalence about the source of life is psychologically un-derstandable without postulating a collective unconscious or an archetype. While the life-giving power of the cosmos does in-deed bring us into the world, it also brings us into the world to die. Everything which is born, dies; everything which comes alive, eventually corrupts. Whoever is responsible for life is also responsible for death. Whoever gives birth also produces that which is dying already. Humankind experiences joy at the birth of a child, but it also realizes that that child is born to die. Real-ity, whatever it is, brings us into being only to take that being

away. Life and death are one. That same elementary dynamism
which creates also destroys. Small wonder, then, that the
woman, the bearer of life, is also seen as the bearer of death.

So we humans are ambivalent about life, but we are also ambivalent about death. We do not have to postulate a death in-
stinct, a *Thanatos,* as did Freud in his later writings, to know that
there are powerful, self-destructive dynamisms in the human
personality. But there are also many times in the course of life
when cares, worries, frustrations, pain become too much and
death appears as a liberation, an escape, a peaceful sleep. So we
are ambivalent about the source of life and the end of life. Both
may look terrible on occasion, and both may also on occasion
look attractive. The Egyptian goddess, Nut, early became the benign goddess of death who embraces the dead man against her
bared breasts and offers him rebirth of a sort. The monster Am-
mit is replaced by the Mother Isis who holds the body of her
dead son in her arms awaiting his rebirth. Even the fierce and
fearsome Kali takes on a benign form, appearing as the goddess
of rebirth and resurrection with her breasts available to provide
nourishment for new life. Tara, the Buddhist transformation of
Kali, represents the most gentle and most peaceful of resurrec-
tions.

The primal chaos is feminine in the typical ancient cosmology.
Creation comes from the slaying of the feminine and the ordering
of its parts by the masculine. But the life-giving forces are still
feminine. When we die, we return to raw creativity; we are destroyed, but we are also reunited. We rot and corrupt, but in that
corruption we are integrated once again with the raw, elementary
forces from which we came. There is, if not joy from this reunion, at least a sense of peace. When we are dead we are freed
from the burdens of life. Death may be a hideous fate, but it may
be also a gentle and peaceful sleep.

So death may be at some times devouring and destructive, at
other times gentle and tender; but at all times it is implicit in the
life-giving forces of the universe. And may not the raw, primal
creativity, which produces us and destroys us, bring us new life
once again? Nut and Tara, at least, suggest that such rebirth is
possible.

There is nothing of the devourer or the destroyer in the New Testament image of Mary. As a corporate personality she represents both Zion, after whom God lusted, and the church, the loving mother of us all. The church surely is not in Christian theory (whatever it may have become in sad actuality) a devouring mother, but it does reintegrate, reunite. Baptism, by which we are initiated into the Church, is a death and rebirth experience in its clear and obvious symbolism. We are buried in the waters of baptism in order that we might rise again purified. We put off the old man in order to put on the new; we die to what we were in order that we might live in Christ Jesus. To come alive in the church one must pass through a kind of death; one must molder in the tomb with Christ (in the waters of baptism) in order that one come alive again with Christ to a new life here on earth as prelude to permanent life in the kingdom with the Father. Mary is the archetype of the Church. She sees us through this spiritual death and presides over our spiritual rebirth. She held the dead body of Jesus in her arms (against her breasts in Christian plastic art, just as did the ancient death goddesses of old). But she held the dead Jesus only as an interlude in preparation for his resurrection. So she accepts us into the earth (as a type of the church) through a temporary process of death from which new life will emerge in Christ Jesus. The church reintegrates humankind by first requiring that individual humans must die in order that they might live again not in suspicion and trust, which separates us from our fellows, but in generous love, which unites us to one another. Mary the Pietà becomes a "goddess" of death insofar as she and her type, the church, presides over the death and rebirth experience of baptism.

The Pietà is the loving mother who presides over the destruction of old life and its renewal in baptism. She is also the loving mother who will preside over the final death and resurrection at the end of our lives, of which baptism is in Christian theory the anticipation and the guarantee. Baptism, St. Paul tells us, is the *arabon*, the down payment, on final resurrection.

There is a striking similarity between Mary the Pietà and Isis or Nut as goddesses of death. All hold a beloved son in their arms in death as a prelude to rebirth; all display the gentle, tender, accepting, reintegrating aspects of death. That which tenderly gave life receives it back again tenderly in death. But there is another side to Mary, the symbol of death, which can certainly be found in popular piety if not in the Scriptures. Mary the mother, like her antetype, the church, can be a fierce and destructive protector of those who assault her children. So various cults of Mary became identified with persecuted and oppressed peoples who sought religious and political freedom. She became also part of the symbols of national identity as well as at times a militant nationalism. Our Lady of Guadalupe was the religious rallying point of Mexican Christians during persecutions, and she survived the decades of religious oppression undiminished. Icons of Mary watch the masters of the Kremlin as they go to and from their daily tasks. The Black Virgin of Czestochowa represents the quintessence of passionate Polish nationalism and religious fidelity. Campostella and Walsingham were once fierce symbols of national identity for Spain and England. Mary was one of those responsible for sending Joan of Arc into battle, and, according to legend and G. K. Chesterton's poem, she inspired a tired and weary Alfred to take up the sword again to do battle with the Danes at White Horse Vale. Many of the IRA "provos" carry the rosary in their pockets.

The image of Mary, then, with the seven swords of sorrow in her heart, but a single sword of militancy, liberation, revolution in her hand, is certainly part of the Christian tradition. The militant, violent, warlike mother who protects her children fiercely may have no basis in Scripture, but it has considerable basis in history and psychology. The militancy, anger, and fury which might be called the "dark side" of the Mary myth is demonstrated, for example, in the anonymous sixteenth-century protest against Cromwell's destruction of the shrine at Walsingham:

> In the wrecks of Walsingham
>   Whom should I choose,
> But the Queen of Walsingham
>   To be guide to my muse?
> Then, thou Prince of Walsingham,
>   Grant me to frame

Bitter plaints to rue thy wrong,
 Bitter woe for thy name.

Bitter was it, on, to see
 The silly sheep
Murdered by the ravening wolves,
 While the shepherds did sleep.
Bitter was it, oh, to view
 The sacred vine,
While the gardeners played all close,
 Rooted up by the swine.
Bitter, bitter, oh, to behold
 The grass to grow
Where the walls of Walsingham
 So stately did show.

Such were the works of Walsingham,
 While she did stand:
Such are the wrecks as now do show
 Of that holy land.
Level, level with the ground
 The towers do lie,
Which, with their golden glittering tops,
 Pierced once the sky.

Where were gates, no gates are now:
 The ways unknown
Where the press of peers did pass,
 While her fame far was blown.
Owls do shriek, where the sweetest hymns
 Lately were sung:
Toads and serpents hold their dens,
 Where the palmers did throng.

Weep, weep, O Walsingham,
 Whose days are nights:
Blessings turned to blasphemies,
 Holy deeds to despites;
Sin is where our Lady sate;
 Heaven turned is to hell:
Satan sits where our Lord did sway—
 Walsingham, oh, farewell.

"A Lament for our Lady's Shrine at Walsingham"—Anonymous.

The shrine is once again established at Walsingham—as it is at Guadalupe and Czestochowa. One may not consider Hilaire Belloc's poetry the acme of expression, but the militant, even belligerent, image of the Church in Mary is fiercely captured in his "Ballade to our Lady of Czestochowa." Mary in the poem is the goddess of death who will receive the battling Hilaire when he dies. She will move him and those who believe as he does "to vengeance in the glories of the bold," in particular against modern politicians who can be bought and sold and who preside over a civilization that is "a crumbling sty."

I

Lady and Queen and Mystery manifold
    And very Regent of the untroubled sky,
Whom in a dream St. Hilda did behold
    And heard a woodland music passing by:
    You shall receive me when the clouds are high
With evening and the sheep attain the fold
This is the faith that I have held and hold,
    And this is that in which I mean to die.

II

Steep are the seas and savaging and cold
    In broken waters terrible to try;
And vast against the winter night the wold,
    And harbourless for any sail to lie.
    But you shall lead me to the lights, and I
Shall hymn you in a harbour story told.
This is the faith that I have held and hold,
    And this is that in which I mean to die.

III

Help of the half-defeated, House of gold,
    Shrine of the Sword, and Tower of Ivory;
Splendour apart, supreme and aureoled,
    The Battler's vision and the World's reply.
    You shall restore me, O my last Ally,
To vengeance and the glories of the bold.
This is the faith that I have held and hold,
    And this is that in which I mean to die.

Envoi

Prince of the degradations bought and sold,
 These verses, written in your crumbling sty,
Proclaim the faith that I have held and hold
 And publish that in which I mean to die.

"Ballade to Our Lady of Czestochowa" by Hilaire Belloc (1870–1953)

Such fiery hymns of the Church Belligerent, not to say the Church Berserk, may seem slightly less than appropriate for our own more irenic age of ecumenism and internationalism. Mary, the "help of Christians," leading John of Austria to victory over the Turks at Leponto seems much more appropriate as a Counter-reformation image than a modern one, so in the remainder of this chapter I shall emphasize the Pietà dimension of Mary the Mother of Sorrows, the Mother of Death, as opposed to the image of Mary the Sword-carrier. It would be a mistake, though, to think that the latter theme is not an authentic part of the tradition of the Mary myth or that it does not reveal something of the fierceness of the church which even in an ecumenical age has a role to play as passionate defender of truth, freedom, and justice. Finally, Mary, the warlike mother, also reflects the deity who for all his love and tenderness can legitimately be thought of as fiercely angry at oppression and injustice, at persecution and suffering and misery. The Yahweh of the Old Testament became furious at the persecution of the innocent; Mary, leading troops into battle, reflects the same aspect of God.

Mary the Reconciler, I think, is a far more pertinent symbol than Mary the Militant Mother who distributes machine guns. Still, there are times when humans must fight, times when reconciliation does not work, times when civil and urbane politics must yield to violence. I would believe that in the present world circumstances reconciliation is a far more appropriate strategy than revolution. Of course, even in the politics of reconciliation and coalition-building, competition, confrontation, and conflict are essential parts of political methodology. Defending human rights, your own and other people's, necessarily involves conflict and confrontation even if it is done within a system which seeks to build an overarching consensus. Mary the fierce, protective mother could surely be thought of as one who presides over struggles for freedom, justice, and dignity. Mary, sword in hand, can appropriately be thought of as a leader of crusades against all evils of oppression, injustice, and bigotry.

Still, by far the stronger aspect of Mary as the goddess of death is the Pietà, the Mother of Sorrows, who receives the dead body of her son into her arms. The human existential need which precedes dialogue with the Pietà symbol is, I think, ambivalence about life. Sometimes our weariness with life is the result of frustration, disappointment, failure. It has become a rut out of which we need to be jarred. But there is a deeper weariness of life which is conveyed in the notion that we are pilgrims wandering through a vale of tears. We are created with a hunger for the ultimate, the absolute; and all imitations become unsatisfactory after a time. We are thrust into being when the reality of our existence is severed from physical integration into the universe. We come into the world crying, in part because we are protesting the indignity of our thrust into being. Neither the time nor the manner of our existence are matters about which we were consulted. So we wander through life hungering, yearning, searching for the absolute, more or less enjoying life, but realizing that the taste of even the greatest pleasures is all too fleeting and only briefly distracts us from our urge to be reunited again with that from which we were sundered by our entering existence as a separate, individuated, person. Our ambivalence about life is essentially the result of our dissatisfaction with the individuation that means separation. We wish that we could be lost again in the great cosmic processes from which we emerged.

The limit-experience which can follow such an existential need is that of dying to the individual self and being absorbed in the cosmic collectivity which can give us a new, more serene and peaceful life. Loss of self is part of any moderately intense religious experience. The mystics tell us that in their moments of ecstasy the "other" (whatever it may be) takes over their personalities and is by far the more real of the two who participate in the encounter. The lonely, anxious, restless, dissatisfied self is almost swept away and absorbed by whatever it is that takes possession. The individuation that began at birth is temporarily suspended. (And it does not follow, as many psychoanalysts argue, that ecstasy is a regression to an infantile state.)

In less dramatic limit-experiences, we also discover the transiency of life and the contingency of the individuated self. The grass will grow up every year on the side of the dune even after I am dead. The trees I plant this autumn will be here long after I am forgotten; beautiful women will still walk down Michigan Avenue; the first vespers of Christmas will still be sung. The cosmic process, the human experience will go on. I am but a grain of sand on the beach, a drop of water in the ocean.

There is something overwhelmingly terrifying about this discovery of the contingency and the temporariness of the individuated self. But there can also be at the same time an experience of great peace and serenity. One takes up life for a brief period and then returns it. It was a loving and benign power which gave us life, it will be a loving and benign power that receives it back. In the experience of something having been given, of oneself as "gifted," there is the impulse to return that which was given generously, freely, serenely; to respond to grace with a gracious gift in exchange. To be separated, to be thrust into being is good, though it is a limited and imperfect good; but to end the separation, to be accepted back into Being is terrifying, yet it also seems to be good. From our realization of contingency there also flows great peace and serenity. We know from research on dying that at least in sudden-death episodes, the final instant is one of peace and serenity bordering on ecstasy. Those who have miraculously survived certain death attest that those moments have had a profound effect on the rest of their lives.

Similarly, those who have had mystical experiences of death, testify that while there is great terror surrounding their experience there is also great peacefulness, relaxation, serenity. If one is freed from the necessity of clinging fearfully to the shreds of being that is the individuated self, the result apparently can be, not defeat and despair but peace and, in fact, a vigorously reconstituted and more relaxed self.

The old structures of perception are shattered by such limit-experiences. Life is something that is not to be clung to; we can care and at the same time not care. There is no need to be panicky, defensive, threatened, insecure. Having "lost" ourselves temporarily to the thing that has invaded us and become a symbol, we emerge with our perceptions restructured, viewing the world and its problems, worries, and troubles with a greater sense of the transiency and contingency of all things. From this improved perspective we are able to give ourselves more effectively to the world, since now we work from peace, not from terror.

In other words, in a limit-experience where we discover our own transiency and contingency, our own reality as being and not Being, we in fact die to the old man and rise to the new. Baptism is intended to be a limit-experience. In the very depths of its symbolism it reminds us of the day we come into Mother Church and that henceforth our life will be brief, and as the waters are poured over our heads, so in the not too distant future, the holy waters will be sprinkled on our caskets. But by the very fact that at baptism we accept the transiency and contingency of our lives, accept the existential limitations of being an *ens ab alio,* we then become free to live with the peace and serenity, the generosity and the openness that have come from resignation. We have learned to care and not to care.

In the limit-experience of obtaining peace and serenity through acceptance of death something else is given. There is another gift, another sacrament, another grace. Having come to terms with ourselves and the finitude of our existence in the arms of the Pietà, and having experienced, astonishingly enough, resurgence of vitality and energy, we encounter the amazing phenomenon of rebirth. Having died, we are reborn; having been baptized, we rise to new life; having died to the old man, we now life to the new man. The acceptance of death does not mean cessation of effort; it means new, more peaceful, better controlled, and more effective effort. Dying, we are reborn.

So what the hell is going on?

There may just be no other limit-experience quite like that one.

> For birth hath in itself the germ of death,
>> But death hath in itself the germ of birth.
> It is the falling acorn buds the tree,
> The falling rain that bears the greenery,

The fern-plants moulder when the ferns arise.
For there is nothing lives but something dies,
And there is nothing dies but something lives.
Till skies be fugitives,
Till Time, the hidden root of change, updries,
Are Birth and Death inseparable on earth;
For they are twain yet one, and Death is Birth.

"Ode to the Setting Sun" by Francis Thompson (1859–1907)

The rhythm between life and death, the periodicity, the alternation is the most baffling of all limit-experiences. One approaches the horizon of one's life, accepts it, and then finds that the horizon has been changed, transformed. Why, once we have accepted death, do we then experience rebirth? What kind of game is being played out there beyond the boundary? Who is shifting the limits around?

Such a limit-experience is not new. Nut and Isis were resurrection goddesses before Mary became the Pietà. All three represent the fundamental human insight that the experience of the acceptance of death paradoxically leads to a sense of rebirth. To link Isis, Nut, and Mary is not to say that the revelations of the three goddesses are exactly the same. It is merely to assert that the Christian conviction of resurrection builds on the limit-experience that is universal in the human condition. Jesus' dead body, which was taken gently and lovingly into the arms of his mother, has risen; and in our experience of the dead and risen Jesus, we encounter the best symbol available to re-present our unshakable conviction that human life does make sense, as well as our paradoxical intuition that death is birth and dying is a prelude to rising again.

For Catholics, the church, the prototype of Mary, is also the Pietà, a loving mother tenderly leading us to a life of repeated deaths and rebirths, and endless progression of putting off the old man and putting on the new in Christ Jesus. As sons and daughters of the church, we die a thousand deaths thoughout our lives in order that we might have a thousand and one rebirths. The church imposes fierce challenges and demands on us; it demands—at least in its better moments—that we live as though we were already in the eschatological age. It requires us to die to our old fears and anxieties, our defenses, our vindictiveness, our cynicism every time we renew baptism as we bless ourselves with holy water. In each new death the church, our Mother, requires of us and also (again, in her better moments) makes available to us rebirth to a new life. We must, as St. Paul says, think of ourselves now as dead to sin but alive to Christ Jesus.

What is revealed to us in the limit experience of accepting death? What is the grace we receive? What is the thing that invades us and becomes the symbol, now also a sacrament? What is going on out there beyond the boundaries? The hint we receive is that the love that brings life, the love that brings renewal, the love that pursues us and seduces us so passionately is also a love which will eventually receive us back into all-embracing unity in which the separateness, the isolation, the alienation of the individuated self is absorbed once again into the totality of Being. But—and here is the core of the paradox of this limit-experience—we also intuit that the love beyond the boundaries, by so absorbing us back into primal unity, will not in fact destroy whatever is most truly us but liberate it and enrich it. The self will not be annihilated but will be transformed. He who loses life shall find it.

One may or may not accept this grace as revealed in the sacrament which is the Pietà. One may accept the paradox of life which bestows death and death which bestows life with great serenity and confidence and never articulate the limit-experience in the limit-language terms of "life after death." But whatever language one uses it is still hard for us cynical, skeptical, cautious, fearful, life-clinging humans to really accept the grace that is given to us in the limit-experience of resignation. It is, of course, only a hint of an explanation, and in that hint very few details are provided. We can refuse to accept the hint because it is too good to be true; it must be wish fulfillment or self-deception. It probably isn't true. But what if it is?

And that is the most basic religious dilemma for humankind.

The illumination that we receive from the Pietà—or from any symbol which plays a similar function in a limit-experience—is one of resignation and peace. It is no longer necessary to be anxious, to be worried. We accept death, and in the peace which comes from that acceptance we are able to live. We are able to care and not to care; and in the serenity born out of the confidence that comes from resignation, we care far more lovingly and far more effectively than we ever did before. We have found the peace that the world cannot give.

So we can turn to the remainder of our lives—fifty years or five minutes—with an attitude of acceptance. We do not abandon our commitments, we do not neglect our obligations, we do not mitigate our celebrations; but we stop worrying. We still change what we can, but we do not become upset about what we cannot change. We love with all the power at our command, but we are not shattered by the discovery of how inadequate and incomplete that love so frequently is. We celebrate with fantasy and festivity, but we are not disheartened when the festivity breaks down and the fantasy ends. We don't especially like it when it rains on our parade, but parades are still good things, rain or shine.

Acceptance and resignation, therefore, do not mean passivity. They are not cop-outs; they do not mean that we turn away from our fellow humans. Rather, we learn from the limit-experience of resignation that all things human are transient and fragile, and that it is foolish to rant and rave about their imperfections. One does what one can while one has time; but one has not failed because the messianic age had not appeared before one's twenty-fifth birthday. Furthermore, one understands that effective action for other human beings does not require high levels of guilt or fear or neurotic anxiety. Indeed, the service of other human beings is far more effective when it is done in a spirit of peace and serenity, when it is done to reflect the graciousness of the universe rather than to do penance for one's own guilt. A man who has been through the limit-experience of losing his individuation and rests in the loving arms and on the soft breasts of the Pietà simply does not believe in neurotic guilt as an effective and sustained motivation for human behavior. Those who consider it necessary to keep guilt levels high in order to change society are merely revealing how desperately they cling to their own transient, contingent individuated self. They think that guilt is necessary to sustain commitment and that commitment defines being. In fact, however, commitment really only begins when guilt is replaced by that peaceful resignation that generates new life. To be effective in one's social commitment one must first of all die to the old self that seeks self-validation through the commitment and rise to the new self which is capable of giving generously to others without any fixation on the self-as-giver. Only when one has lost one's self can one make the gift of self. He who loses his life shall find it. More than that, he shall be able to give it.

Mary, having lost everything that mattered to her at the foot of the cross, was then able to give herself to the whole of humankind: "Son, behold thy mother."

Such generous, resigned, peaceful giving of oneself is absolutely essential in the intimate relationship between man and woman. He who goes into marriage to validate his masculinity or she who enters it to validate her femininity is bound to be frustrated. For in marriage you do not seek something you don't have; you rather seek to give something you already possess. One priest I know hopes he will be able to marry eventually, because, he says, before he dies he wants to have someone to love him. Wanting to have someone love you is indeed an admirable goal, but it is not a good reason for getting married. On the contrary, the only reason for getting married that makes much sense is that you want to love someone else. One marries not to possess but to be possessed.

Intimacy, to be successful, requires acceptance, resignation, peacefulness, the loss of self which is an absolute prerequisite for the discovery of the self. In a happy marriage both husband and wife must die to their old selves in order to be born again. The new selves they discover in the interchange and the dialectic of their relationship will join in the Pietà at the foot of the cross in surrender of their old stubborn, tenacious, vindictive styles of keeping other humans at bay. They must sweep away the protective shield of their defense mechanisms and become vulnerable to one another. In the limit-experience of accepting death, one radically and profoundly accepts one's own total vulnerability as being; one recognizes not merely that it is possible to get hurt but that one will get hurt and will be ultimately hurt in death. Then one is able to risk being hurt in intimate union with another. More than that, one knows that one will be hurt and, lamentably, one will also hurt; but it does not end there. For if you resign yourself to the inevitability of being hurt, you also acquire peace, serenity, confidence, self-possession, and you can give yourself to another and accept the other in return. One will be hurt, but one will have joy; one will have joy, but one will be reborn. The tears will come, but they will be wiped away in joy. To protect one's vulnerability is to prevent injury, but then one cannot be possessed. If one cannot be possessed, one is quite incapable of possessing.

In the limit-experience of resignation and acceptance, one lays life down gladly and generously. In human intimacy one not only dies to the old, selfish, separated self, one dies for the other person, the other who has lured one into the snare of intimacy and promises a rebirth, a new life, if only one will give oneself to the total vulnerability of death. Intimacy is a limit-experience in the strict sense of the word. In the other who demands that we die that we both might live is the advance agent of that Other who is lurking behind the boundary wall of life itself. I think that second Other claps his hands with joy when we are first beguiled into her/his tender trap and brings us to death and rebirth in the seductive clasp of intimate human relationship.

The theme of sorrow turned into joy has been echoed repeatedly in poetry. John Mauropus, a Greek poet of the eleventh century, sings of the Lady of the Passion:

> O Lady of the Passion, dost thou weep?
> What help can we then through our tears survey,
> If such as thou a cause for wailing keep?
> What help, what hope, for us, sweet Lady, say?
> "Good man, it doth befit thine heart to lay
> More courage next it, having seen me so.
> All other hearts find other balm today,—
> *The Whole world's Consolation is my woe!"*

> "Our Lady of the Passion" by John Mauropus.
> Translated from the Greek by Elizabeth Barrett Browning

Two hundred years later, the Franciscan bard Jacapone da Todi wrote the famous *Stabat Mater,* whose thundering Latin verses have lost much of their power, alas, for those of us who had to hear them sung badly during those seemingly endless Stations of the Cross services in which we were imprisoned through all our years of Catholic schooling on Fridays in Lent. Still they are magnificent and ought to be listened to:

> Virgin holiest, Virgin purest,
> Of that anguish thou endurest
>   Make me bear with thee my part;
> Of his passion bear the token
> In a spirit bowed and broken,
>   Bear his death within my heart.
>
> May his wounds both wound and heal me;
> His blood enkindle, cleanse, anneal me;
>   Be his cross my hope and stay:
> Virgin, when the mountains quiver,
> From that flame which burns for ever,
>   Shield me on the judgment-day.
>
> Christ, when he that shaped me calls me,
> When advancing death appals me,
>   Through her prayer and storm make calm:
> When to dust my dust returneth
> Save a soul to thee that yearneth;
>   Grant it thou the crown and palm.

> *Stabat Mater* by Jacapone da Todi (1128–1306)
> Translated from the Latin by A. de Vere

An anonymous sixteenth-century author echoes the theme of the mixture of suffering and joy:

> The holly and ivy,
> When they are both full grown,
> Of all the trees that are in the wood,
> The holly bears the crown:
>   The rising of the sun
>   And the running of the deer,
>   The playing of the merry organ,
>   Sweet singing in the choir.

The holly bears a blossom,
As white as the lily flower,
And Mary bore sweet Jesus Christ
To be our Saviour:

REFRAIN

The holly bears a berry,
As red as any blood,
And Mary bore sweet Jesus Christ
To do poor sinners good:

The holly bears a prickle
As sharp as any thorn,
And Mary bore sweet Jesus Christ
On Christmas day in the morn:

The holly bears a bark,
As bitter as any gall,
And Mary bore sweet Jesus Christ
For to redeem us all:

The holly and the ivy,
When they are both full grown,
Of all the trees that are in the wood,
The holly bears the crown:

The rising of the sun
And the running of the deer,
The playing of the merry organ,
Sweet singing in the choir.

Rudyard Kipling, of all people, pictured the soldier praying to
Mary, Lady of Sorrows, before going into battle:

O Mary, pierced with sorrow
  Remember, reach and save
The soul that goes tomorrow
  Before the God that gave;
As each was born of woman,
  For each, in utter need
True comrade and brave foeman,
Madonna, intercede.

"O Mary Pierced with Sorrow" by Rudyard Kipling
(1865–1936), from *Song Before Action*

And Giovanni Pecci, who became Pope Leo XIII, wrote an absolutely fierce war cry to Mary in which the warrior queen is depicted as protecting her children from death. Transformation is involved in the poem, but there is little of the Pietà left in it.

> When warfare blusters at high Lucifer's command,
> And writhing monsters fume a course from Acheron's land,
> With speed of wind and wing, O loving Mother haste!
> Shield for the plagued of soul, sword for the heart laid waste!
> Crush with thy virgin foot these cobras of the night,
> Erect thy son a tower on the Mary-height
> Where he may watch the serpents leave, as stars in flight.

> "War Cry: To Mary" (*Ardet pugna ferox; Lucifer ipse, videns*)
> by Leo XIII (1810–1905).
> Translated from the Latin by Raymond F. Roseliep.

In the plastic arts, there is a superabundance of riches, beginning of course with Michelangelo's defaced but now restored Pietà in St. Peter's. It is perhaps one of the greatest works of sculpture ever produced in the world. The sorrow, resignation, and serenity of Mary are also brilliantly depicted by Giotto, Fra Angelico, Van der Weyden, Rembrandt, Rubens, Grünewald, and Gauguin. I must confess that I find many of these *Mater Dolorosas* a bit offensive. Van der Weyden's version is collapsed into the ground, Ruben's has lost all self-control, Grünewald's looks like she is about ready to die herself, Rembrandt's *Mary at the Foot of the Cross* is on the verge of collapse. As far as my own piety and devotion goes, I much prefer the splendid *Our Lady of Sorrows* of Luis Morales, in which one sees a strong, brave, self-possessed woman accepting death, yet already, despite her sorrow, she is experiencing rebirth. Similarly, El Greco's two *Mater Dolorosas* are much more persuasive; the one in Munich is shattered but still strong, and the one in Strasburg is perhaps a little too self-possessed, too determined. Even Gauguin's sickly green virgin combines strength and peace with her sorrow.

With the exception of some of the overwhelmed and collapsing late Renaissance Pietàs, the women depicted at the foot of the cross in most Christian art are deep, deep in sorrow yet able to cope. They have suffered a terrible loss, but they have not lost their faith. They have plunged into the depths, but they are strong enough to rise up. The are resigned; they have accepted. Despite their sorrow, they are in the process of being born again, anticipating, as it were, the resurrection of their son. This is what the limit-experience of acceptance is all about, and what Mary as Pietà—the church, our loving mother—is supposed to represent to all her followers.

> I left a lei, Lady,
>> To say goodby
> Before we sailed away
>> To where men die,
> And vowed to bead on my return
>> Fresh buds for dry.
>
> Should I return not, Lady,
>> When battles cease,
> Grant my vow and promise
>> Sweet release,
> And lay your leis where I lie,
>> And peace.

"Lady of Peace" *Cathedral: Honolulu* by Fra Angelico Chavez (1910–   )

PIETÀ

Experience of Sexual Differentiation	Woman as source of what lives only to die
Biological Origin	Death in arms of beloved
Cognate Symbols	Gate, lock, raven, vulture
Ancient Goddesses	Nut, Kali, Hecate, Isis
Type	Church, the new Zion
Mary Symbol	Pietà
Existential Need	Futility of life, separation
Limit-Experience	Loss of self in resignation to death
Grace that is Given	A love which draws all together back into unity—death as a prelude to new life
Illumination—Restructuring of Perceptions	Peace, serenity.

Action	Acceptance
Man-Woman Implication	Loss of self to another
Poem	Da Todi's *Stabat Mater*
Plastic Art	Michelangelo's *Pietà*

Part VI

ENVOI

NOTRE MÈRE DE LA PLAGE GRAND

I'm sorry, Ma'am, about those clothes
Blue and white and awful rose
And I'm sorry about the color of the snake
Who so fascinates small fry here abouts

"Why does that lady
Stand on that ugly snake?"
They'll not hear a word from me
About what means old Genesis, Chapter Three

But they don't make great statues any more
And if you are to watch over my garden
I had to take what I could get
And worry about the winter cold

"Our Lady of Wicker Park," they say
But that's an ethnic joke
And we don't believe in those
No group to blame for that sickly rose

So you preside over the stormy lake
The Irish kids, the barking dogs
The roaring motors, the golden sails
My dubious flowers and next door
The great show of lights
Which illumine the weekend nights

A long way from Galilee
And a much bigger lake
Chartres this place is not,
I'm sorry, Ma'am, it's all we've got

My friends are baffled
Why *you* of all people
They don't know about the call
From the lofty New York Times

Not much left to the poor Roman Church
But the only female deity still around
God is woman as well as man
The one who creates also calls
The one who orders also touches

The one who plans also entices
The one who judges also consoles

Silly superstition? Only to the rigid
Caught in dogma's bind
Creepy devotion? Only to the dull
Trapped in dismal fear

She who came long before the dynamo
And, if needs be, will live long beyond
Mother, wife, muse, morning star
A revelation of God's warming charms
To a cold and bitter world

Not yet time, perhaps, Lady dear
For new spires to climb the skies
But still reign over our poor Grand Beach
(which is no longer beach or grand)
And wait the certain day
When the hymns begin again

And while we wait
I'll not forget
That here on sandy dunes
I, weary and spent,
Worn and beat,
Found you once again.

A.M.G.

Chapter 9

OUR LIGHT, OUR
SWEETNESS, OUR HOPE?

The wide streams go their way,
The pond lapses back into a glassy silence.
The cause of God in me—has it gone?
Do these bones live? Can I live with these bones?
Mother, Mother of us all, tell me where I am! *

R eligion is a system of symbols which purports to illuminate and provide direction for humans as they wrestle
with the most basic and fundamental ambiguities in life.
Symbols take their origin in limit-experiences in which a person
brushes up against the boundaries, reaches the horizon of his
own existence, and encounters a grace, a sense of something
gifted or given. The limit-experience occurs when we permit a
thing (which can also be a person) to invade our consciousness
and become a symbol, a sacrament, which speaks to us of the
limits of our existence and offers the grace which seems to lurk
somehow or other just beyond the limits. In such an experience
the thing-turned-symbol shatters the old structures of our perception and organizes them into new and different constellations
in which we see things more clearly, more profoundly, more
penetratingly. The thing-turned-symbol incarnates our limit-ex-

* "What Can I Tell My Bones?" copyright © 1957 by Theodore Roethke from *The
Collected Poems of Theodore Roethke*. Reprinted by permission of Doubleday &
Company, Inc. and Faber and Faber Ltd.

perience so that we can recall it to our own memory and share it with others. The religious symbols of the great traditions represent the limit-experience of their founders, and enable those who come after them to share the same limit-experience, to receive the same grace as the founders did. But the great symbols serve not merely to link the experience of the founders to our own experience, they also serve as channels of communication in the opposite direction. We are able through the great symbols to link our own limit-experiences, which are necessarily as unique and special as each of us is, with the experiences of those who began our heritage and who have transmitted it to us. The great symbol makes the original experience present to us, preconditions us for our own experience, and then links the grace which is given to us with the graces that have gone before us.

The sheer density of the being of any thing makes it multilayered and polyvalent. If there are some primal things which in all cultures seem to become religious, the thing itself is sufficiently ambiguous so that the limit-experience by which the thing becomes symbol can have different and even contrary meanings in given religious traditions. Furthermore, the great symbols of any tradition will be more richly and fully understood as different generations of believers discover fuller and broader implications in them. To put the matter differently, as each generation has its own limit-experiences from within its own context and perspective, it reinterprets the great symbol which overarches the culture itself.

The result of the radical restructuring of our perceptions that is caused by a thing-turned-symbol in a limit-experience moves us to neither thought nor reflection but to action. Seeing things differently than we did before our existential crisis began, we necessarily modify our behavior, our response to reality in the light of our now fundamentally different way of perceiving reality. It is only when we begin to reflect on our new behavior that we try to describe the experience, to explain the symbol, to share the experience with others through the symbol. When we do so, we necessarily fall back on limit-language (even if our reflections take the form of philosophical theology). The language of paradox, tension, and intensification to which the ordinary rules of language and interpretation are no longer pertinent characterizes limit-language which seeks to describe the horizons of existence. The limit-experience is odd, out of the ordinary; it can only be described by odd language, language out of the ordinary. A religious symbol which can be expressed in a proposition that does not have at least an implicit paradox will turn out to be a very inadequate symbol.

The process can be described (though somewhat artificially) in the circle of Figure 1 (page 64). A "thing" intrudes itself into our consciousness in response to an existential need. It produces an "experience" that restructures our perceptions and turns the "thing" into a "symbol." The "symbol" in its turn leads to a modification of "action," and that modification is reflected in "limit-language," which purports to state something important about the ultimate nature of human existence, thus providing us with "meaning" by which we can interpret the ambiguities of life. Within the frame of reference which that meaning gives us we can turn to the "thing" again for a regeneration of the "experience."

This cycle is repeated in both the individual person and in the history of religious tradition. Each time a person or a tradition goes through the cycle, new dimensions of the grace revealed by the symbol are experienced. New aspects of the sacrament invade our personality; new meanings "in front" of the symbol are perceived; new and richer language is required to express the experience, the symbol, and the grace revealed.

There are a number of advantages to this mode of religious reflection (or, if one wishes, theological method). Put together from language theology, existential and process philosophy, history of religion, and sociology, it enables one to bypass many of the controversies of the past which are no longer pertinent to our present situation. Two of the age-old problems which have plagued Christian theologians are resolved, or at least become resolvable: the questions of development of doctrine and of the striking similarity of some aspects of Christianity with religions that preceded it and surround it.

Human religious experience is seen as having both unity (based on the fundamentally similar structures of all basic human experiences—light, dark, sun, moon, male, female, birth, death) and a wide diversity (based on the dissimilar modalities by which these things become symbols). Furthermore, since even the great symbols of a religious heritage will trigger different limit-experiences in different times and places, there is room for growth in understanding of the riches of the symbol. It is not so much that we experience Jesus or Mary, let us say, in a unique and special way and thereby get back to what the experience meant to the earliest Christians; it is rather that we, through the symbol and the limit-language passed on to us by our predecessors, experience Jesus and Mary again; and in that experience we get at the meaning "in front" of the symbol, coming to understand the grace revealed in Jesus and Mary in ways that our predecessors could not understand because they did not bring to the experience what we do. Of course we must also acknowledge that our predecessors may have brought to the experiences capacities to perceive that we lack.

The development of doctrine should not be thought of as an evolutionary process in which new and more valuable insights are acquired while the old ones are discarded. Neither can a symbol be interpreted to mean anything the interpreter wants it to mean. A symbol has an integrity and a vitality of its own. There must be a fundamental similarity in the limit-experience produced by the symbol today and the experience the same symbol produced in our predecessors. One must, to put the matter scripturally, experience the same Lord Jesus who had died and risen. If our experience denies the fundamental theme of the experience of our predecessors, it may indeed be splendid, but it is not part of the same heritage, and it is not a response to the illumination of a great symbol of that heritage. If the language we use to describe the limit-experience, which we claim was triggered and formed by a symbol out of our heritage, destroys the basic paradox of the original limit-language, then it is not the same experience or the same symbol. If in the Christian tradition the paradoxes of the crucified-risen God-man, three-one, and virgin-mother are explained away, then one no longer has Christianity. If the new language we attempt to use lacks paradox, it is not limit-language at all and we are not describing limit-experience. Indeed, we are no longer engaged in anything which could properly be called religious.

The greatest disadvantage in this mode of religious reflection is that it is completely different from the mode of religious reflection in which most of us were raised. We have to bracket temporarily the "method" that was assumed in our religious education and which has become the unquestioned and unrecognized context of our religious thought. To let new insights and assumptions develop in an altered context free from that which was instilled in us when we were young is extremely difficult. We try to twist and distort our perceptions and insights to fit the old categories, the old styles of thought. Then we are comforted, for now we can understand the new in terms of the old and as nothing more than a restatement of St. Thomas's "Five Ways" or St. Anselm's ontological argument, for example.

An alternative to this way of encountering something new in the way of religious reflection is to content oneself with identifying it with a heresy out of the past. The new method is nothing more than Schleiermacher or the modernists or Scotus, and so one can write it off.

I think there are distinct advantages to this method of religious reflection. One can apply it rather easily to all the fundamental symbols of the Christian faith. It will take great patience, of course, to analyze the symbols within a multidisciplinary approach. Perhaps more to the point, the method, once grasped, can be used with considerable effectiveness in preaching and teaching. Indeed, those who have tried it in one form or another report that the reaction of the faithful is uniformly positive, particularly because the method breaks down the artificial distinction between "old church" and "new church" or "preconciliar Catholicism" and "postconciliar Catholicism." It is relatively easy also to show people what it is they "always believed" in the expression of a religious doctrine and how that is not only not denied but reinforced and better understood by our new ways of expressing it. The method concentrates, in other words, on the organic continuity between the old and the new and not on the radical discontinuity. (Of course, showing continuity is bound to be offensive to those immature preachers and teachers who believe it is their function to assault and shatter the faith of those who did not receive the superior theological training they had. Such people arrogate to themselves the perception-shattering function which belongs to the symbol itself.)

Another disadvantage of the method is that to pause and reflect on our own religious lives—as opposed to intellectualizing about religion—is the way a religious life really grows and develops. If one thinks about the cycle of religious change and maturation that has gone on within one's own personality, then the schema of Figure 1 acquires a certain rough and intuitive validity. The laity I know who have been introduced to this method seem to "feel" its rightness and are stimulated by it.

There is a final, and from the religious and theological viewpoint perhaps secondary, advantage. This mode of religious reflection is shaped by the social sciences in part and also feeds back into further social science research. My colleague William McCready and I have been studying religion as a meaning system. We have tried to get beyond such peripheral (it seems to us) measures as church attendance, denominational affiliation, and the acceptance of doctrinal propositions to the basic worldview with which each person approaches the primal poignancy, ambiguities, and problems of human life. We have also, coincidentally, been studying religious experiences. We have just recently grasped the relationship between religion as meaning system and symbol as expression of limit-experience. In further research we will have to link the two, and we will also have to explore, not just the ecstatic limit-experiences but much more ordinary and commonplace limit-experiences. It is apparent to us now that a sociology of religion which is not concerned with the "ordinary" limit-experiences of everyday life will not even begin to cope with what religion means to either the individual human person or the collectivity of human society.

This book is an attempt to apply this mode of religious reflection to the great symbol of Catholic Christianity, Mary, the virgin mother of Jesus. Mary is the Catholic Christian religion's symbol which reveals to us that the Ultimate is androgynous, that in God there is both male and female, both pursuit and seduction, both ingenious plan and passionate tenderness. Mary is the Christian symbol which incarnates the experience of sexual differentiation as sacrament, as grace revealing Something or Someone beyond the horizons of our life, beyond the limits of daily existence. Sexual differentiation has been a source of limit-experience and religious meaning since the beginning of anything we might know as human culture. Mary is the life-giving mother, the life-renewing virgin, the attractive and fascinating Daughter of Zion, and the reuniting, peace-giving Pietà. She reveals to us the feminine dimensions of the Christian God, and at the same time reinforces our perceptions of all things, including ourselves, as androgynous in some fashion.

This exercise may be summed up in table form. (See page 221) I would make two comments on the table. First, there is a reciprocating interaction between the experience of sexual differentiation, the limit-experience, and the Mary symbol. Not all experiences of sexual differentiation become limit-experience; most do not. Similarly, by no means is sex the only thing which can turn a limit-experience into a symbol. Second, there are other symbols besides Mary which can trigger limit-experiences, whether they arise out of the perception of sexual differentiation or from the perception of some other thing that is potentially a symbol.

Thus there is no necessary linkage between the three rows in the table labeled Experience of Sexual Differentiation, Mary Symbol, and Limit-Experience. There is a strain toward a close connection, however. The experience of sexual love is surely one of the most powerful of the potential limit-experiences available to humankind. Furthermore, for most people sexual love is likely to be the most intense if not the only limit-experience in their lives. It is also true, of course, that the nature of the limit-experience is such that it readily admits of description in sexual terms—being attracted, invaded, taken over, surrendering, and taking possession of. It is not only the great mystics who have fallen back onto sexual imagery to describe their ecstatic limit-experiences. Anyone who knows what it is like to give oneself over to the contemplation of a thing-becoming-symbol sees the sexual overtones and implications of absorbing that thing unto oneself.

Finally, because sexual differentiation can so easily become limit-experience, and because limit-experience so easily takes on sexual connotation, a religious symbol based on a great tradition's perception of the sacramental and revelatory grace of sexual differentiation readily becomes both a trigger for limit-experience (sexual or otherwise, but especially sexual) and a means of articulating such experience.

Mary—Madonna, Virgo, Sponsa, Pietà—is a natural trigger for a limit-experience of any kind (in the sense that she creates a context and ambience in which in our existential need we can turn to a thing and let it become symbol). She is also a readily available instrument for describing to others what went on in the experience. Other religious symbols can do the same thing, of course, and often have. I only suggest that Mary, the Christian mother goddess, is an obvious and natural symbol to reflect the femininity which is blended with masculinity in the androgynous God. She is the natural trigger for and expression of sexual differentiation which becomes a grace, a sacrament, a revelation. I also argue that it is inherent in the Mary symbol that she be seen as "presiding over" the limit-experience of sexual love as reflecting God's furious and tender passion for his human creatures. This meaning may be "in front of" the symbol, but it is surely not extrinsic to it. Indeed, particularly in marriage liturgies and marriage customs, it has not been unrecognized in the past.

For the purposes of description it has been necessary to separate in analysis that which is always united in reality. In any experience of a member of the opposite sex that is at all rich or full, all the elements of sexual differentiation are experienced as a totality. One does not see a woman as eyes, breasts, vulva, or womb. One sees the whole person. Mary is Madonna, Virgo, Sponsa, Pietà all at once. One does not experience maternity distinct from inspiration, inspiration distinct from arousal, and arousal distinct from tender consolation. They all happen at the same time. If we select one image from among the others, it is only because that particular image is most obvious in the given set of circumstances. So, too, are the existential problems—discouragement, despair, futility, isolation, restriction, separation, weariness—are all experienced together, though usually one or a few may dominate. Also, in any limit-experience worthy of the name we encounter life being given, life being renewed, life demanding abandonment, and life reuniting us to the cosmos all at once. And the God, or the Ultimate, or Whoever, is always experienced simultaneously as passionately tender, implacably faithful, seductively attractive, and tenderly consoling. So, too, we emerge from a limit-experience (unless we resist the "givenness" and the "gifted-ness" which such an experience attempts to impose upon us) with a combination of hope, trust, freedom, and peace. One grace, one revelation, one emotion may stand out more sharply than the others, but all are present. Mary is Madonna, Virgo, Sponsa, Pietà. Mary is Woman; and that says it all.

What does woman do to man? (Or, alternately, what does man do to woman?) In the language of modern idiom, they "turn each other on." When we are "turned on" by a member of the opposite sex, we are transformed. The whole idea is that God wants to turn us on. He (She, It, They) wants to remake us. If the Mary symbol has any meaning at all, then it tells us that God prays in a fashion not unlike these words from Roethke's poem, "Meditation of an Old Woman":

> How I wish them awake!
> May the high flower of the hay climb into their hearts;
> May they lean into light and live;
> May they sleep in robes of green, among the ancient ferns;
> May their eyes gleam with the first dawn;
> May the sun gild them like a worm;
> May they be taken by the true burning;
> May they flame into being! *

May we flame into being. Well, that's not a bad idea.

But what are the chances for the one about whom I write? Can she tell us where we are, and even more important, where we should be going? Can she possibly survive in a world that has been variously described as heading for ecological apocalypse and destroyed by a "liberated," "permissive" culture? Is the Lady of Bethlehem an anachronism?

* "Old Woman's Meditation," copyright © 1955 by Theodore Roethke, from *The Collected Poems of Theodore Roethke*. Reprinted by permission of Doubleday & Company, Inc. and Faber and Faber Ltd.

Maybe. Still, if it comes to a competition between Heilbroner's Atlas and Adams's smiling Virgin of Chartres, I think I can venture a bet as to which of the two will win.

> Blessed sister, holy mother, spirit of the fountain,
>   spirit of the garden,
> Suffer us not to mock ourselves with falsehood
> Teach us to care and not to care
> Teach us to sit still
> Even among these rocks,
> Our peace in His will
> And even among these rocks
> Sister, mother
> And spirit of the river, spirit of the sea,
> Suffer me not to be separated
>
> And let my cry come unto Thee.*

T. S. Eliot, "Ash Wednesday"

Four Aspects of Mary

	MADONNA	VIRGO	SPONSA	PIETÀ
Experience of Sexual Differentiation	Maternity	Transforming, inspiring, renewing	Pleasure, lust	Woman as source of what lives only to die
Biological Origin	Birth, nursing, taking care	Arousal, heightened consciousness	Orgasm	Death in arms of beloved
Cognate Symbols	Earth, water (womb), home, hearth	Moon, lotus, lily	Moon, planets (Venus)	Gate, lock, raven, vulture
Ancient Goddesses	Isis, Demeter, Juno	Shakti, Kwan-yin, Sophia, Tara	Venus, Astarte, Aphrodite	Nut, Kali, Hecate, Isis
Type	Eve, the source of life	Eve, the beginning	Daughter of Zion	Church, the new Zion
Mary Symbol	Madonna	Virgin full of grace	Sponsa, desired of Yahweh (corporate personality in NT)	Pietà
Existential Need	Discouragement, despair	Weariness	Aloneness, isolation, restriction, inhibition	Futility of life, separation
Limit-Experience	Vitality of cosmos, life-giving love	Renewal, transformation	Passionate abandon	Peace, serenity
Grace that is Given	Inexhaustible and passionate tenderness of life-giving love	Implacable fidelity of life-giving love, which is also life-renewing	A love that pursues and attracts, invades and tempts	A love which draws all together back into unity—death as a prelude to new life
Illumination—Restructuring perceptions	Hope	Trust	Freedom	Peace, serenity
Action	Protection and improvement of the earth (Mary's garden)	Commitment	Celebration	Acceptance
Man-Woman Implication	Acceptance of androgyny	Both man and woman can inspire, renew, and surrender to inspiration and renewal	Playful pleasure	Loss of self to another
Poem	May Magnificat (Hopkins)	Seraph of Heaven (Shelley)	Dialogue between Mary and Gabriel (Auden)	Stabat Mater (da Todi)
Plastic Art	Michelangelo's Holy Family	El Greco's The Assumption	Botticelli's Annunciation	Michelangelo's Pietà

Figure II: *The Religious Cycle in the Individual and in a Tradition*

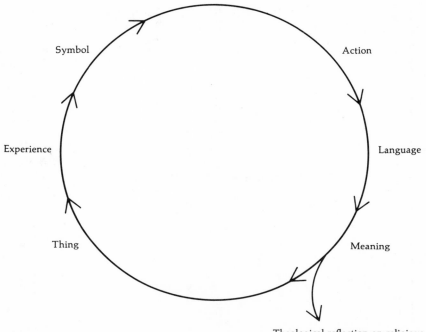

Theological reflection on religious
meaning (may occur, but not
essential for the individual)

NOTES

Chapter 1

1. Robert Heilbroner, *An Inquiry into the Human Prospect*. New York: W. W. Norton & Company, Inc., 1974, p. 15.

2. Ibid., p. 70.

3. Ibid., p. 144.

4. Loren Eiseley, *The Firmament of Time*. New York: Atheneum, 1960; Richard Goodwin, *The American Condition*, New York: Doubleday & Co., 1973; Peter Schrag, *The End of the American Future*, New York: Simon and Schuster, 1973, and *Man's Eight Deadly Sins*, New York: Harcourt Brace, 1974.

5. Theodore Roszak, *Where the Wasteland Ends: Politics and Transcendence in Post-Industrial Society*. Garden City, New York: Doubleday & Co., 1972.

6. Lynn White, Jr., *Machina Ex Deo: Essays in the Dynamism of Western Culture*. Cambridge; Massachusetts Institute of Technology Press, 1969.

7. Harvey Cox, *The Seduction of the Spirit*. New York: Simon & Schuster, 1973.

8. Ibid.

9. Charles Dickson, "Mariology: A Protestant Reconsideration" in *American Ecclesiastical Review* (May 1974), pp. 306–7.

10. See, for example, John McHugh, *The Mother of Jesus in the New Testament*. London: Barton, Longman & Todd, 1974; Lucien Deiss, *Mary Daughter of Zion*, Collegeville, Minn.: Liturgical Press, 1972; Raymond Brown, *The Virginal Conception & Bodily Resurrection of Jesus*, New York: Paulist Press, 1973; and also the excellent commentary on the Cana incident and the dialogue at the foot of the cross in Raymond Brown's, *The Gospel According to St. John*, Volumes 29 and 29A, New York: Doubleday & Co., Anchor Bible, 1966 and 1970.

11. Karl Rahner, *Mary, Mother of the Lord*, New York: Herder and Herder, 1963; Hugo Rahner, *Our Lady and the Church*, New York: Pantheon Books, 1961; Yves Congar, *Christ, Our Lady, and the Church*, Westminster, Maryland: The Newman Press, 1957; Rene Laurentin, *The Question of Mary*, New York: Holt, Rinehart and Winston, 1965; Edward Schillebeeckx, *Mary, Mother of the Church*, New York: Sheed & Ward, 1964; Otto Semelroth, *Mary, Archetype of the Church*, New York:

Sheed & Ward, 1963; Max Thurian, *Mary, Mother of All Christians,* New York: Herder and Herder, 1964.

12. Juniper P. Carol, *Mariology,* Vols. I, II, III. Milwaukee: Bruce Publishing Company, 1961; F. J. Sheed, *The Mary Book,* New York: Sheed & Ward, 1950; Hilda Graef, *Mary: A History of Doctrine and Devotion,* Vols. I, II, New York: Sheed & Ward, 1965.

13. Sister M. Therese, *I Sing of a Maiden: The Mary Book of Verse,* New York: Macmillan, 1947; Henri Gheon, *The Madonna in Art,* Paris: Tisne, 1947, and *Mary Mother of God,* Chicago: Henry Regnery Company, 1955; Jean Guiton, *Images de la Vierge,* Paris: Editions Sun, 1963.

NOTE: I wish to thank in particular Bishop Thomas Grady and Sister Candida Lund and the library of Rosary College in River Forest, Illinois, for supplying me with these materials.

14. Clifford Geertz, "Religion as a Cultural System," in Donald Cutler (ed.), *The Religious Situation: 1968,* Boston: Beacon Press, 1968, and *Islam Observed,* New Haven: Yale University Press, 1969; Thomas Luckmann, *The Invisible Religion,* New York: Macmillan, 1967; Andrew M. Greeley, *Unsecular Man,* New York: Schocken Books, 1972.

15. Mircea Eliade, *Patterns in Comparative Religion,* New York: Sheed & Ward, 1958; *Myth and Reality,* New York: Harper & Row, 1963; *Myths, Dreams and Mysteries,* New York: Harper & Row, 1960; *The Quest: History and Meaning in Religion,* Chicago: University of Chicago Press, 1969; *The Two and the One,* New York: Harper & Row, 1965; Erich Neumann, *Amor and Psyche: The Psychic Development of the Feminine—A Commentary on the Tale by Apuleius,* translated by Ralph Manheim, Princeton, N.J.: Princeton University Press, Bollingen series 54, 1960; and *The Great Mother: An Analysis of the Archetype,* translated by Ralph Manheim, Princeton, N.J.: Princeton University Press, Bollingen Series 47, 2nd edition, 1963.

16. Langdon Gilkey, *Naming the Whirlwind,* Indianapolis: Bobbs-Merrill, 1969; Paul Ricouer, *The Symbolism of Evil,* Translated by Emerson Buchanan, Boston: Beacon Press, 1967; Peter Berger, *A Rumor of Angels,* Garden City, N.Y.: Doubleday, 1969; Nathan A. Scott, *The Wild Prayer of Longing: Poetry and the Sacred,* New Haven: Yale University Press, 1971; Thomas Fawcett, *The Symbolic Language of Religion,* London: S.C.M. Press, 1970; Ian Ramsey, *Religious Language,* London: S.C.M. Press, 1957; David Tracy, *Blessed Rage for Order: The New Pluralism in Theology,* New York: Seabury Press, 1975.

Chapter 2

1. For an alternative approach, see William C. McCready, *Report on Ultimate Values.* Beverly Hills: Sage Press, Sage Library of Social Research, 1975.

2. Geertz, *Religion as Cultural System,* p. 643.

3. See my book, *Ecstasy: A Way of Knowing,* Englewood Cliffs, N.J.: Prentice-Hall, Inc., 1974.

4. David Tracy, *Blessed Rage for Order.*

5. From *The Beautiful Changes and Other Poems,* Harcourt, Brace Jovanovich, Inc., 1947.

6. Thomas Fawcett, *Symbolic Language,* p. 174.

7. Ibid., p. 174.

8. Ibid., p. 170.

9. Ibid., p. 172.

10. Tracy, *Blessed Rage for Order*, Chap. 6.

11. Ibid.

12. Ibid., Chap. 4.

13. For a discussion of this use of the word "grace," see Joseph Sitler, *Essays on Nature and Grace*, Philadelphia: Fortress Press, 1972.

Chapter 3

1. See Mircea Eliade, *Patterns in Comparative Culture*, pp. 420–424.

2. Ibid., pp. 420–21.

3. Ibid., p. 421.

4. There is at least a trace of this in Christianity. Blessed Juliana of Norwich (not exactly whom one would call a feminist) referred to God as "Our loving Mother."

5. Alan Watts, *The Two Hands of God*, New York: George Braziller, 1963. Watts also suggests that the swastika (in the opposite direction of that used by the Nazis) and the filot, as well as the familiar Chinese circle with the two stylized fish, represent the unity of the primordial pair.

6. Ibid., p. 63.

7. Eliade, *The Two and the One*, New York: Harper & Row, 1965, p. 104.

8. Ibid., p. 106.

9. Ibid., p. 106.

10. Ibid., p. 106.

11. Ibid., p. 107.

12. Ibid., p. 107.

13. Ibid., p. 104.

14. Ibid., p. 82.

15. And I hereby repudiate all attempts to shock and scandalize ordinary parishioners by changing the gender of God in religious devotions. Whatever one may do in one's own personal prayer life, one does not reverse two thousand years of custom on a single Sunday morning.

16. Johann Jacob Bachhofen *Das Mutterrecht*, Basle: Gesammelte Werk, Vols. 1–4, 1948–1954.

17. Erich Neumann, *The Great Mother*, p. 94. Plates mentioned here refer to this book.

18. Ibid., pp. 104–105.

19. A reason for the annual orgy, perhaps in addition to uniting the tribe with the rebirth of fertility in springtime, was to set aside a time of the year when passions could be given free reign so that there would be less reason to throw the tribe into a state of sexual disorganization during the rest of the year, hence "carnival"—*carni-valle*, "farewell to the flesh."

20. Let me quickly assert to the feminist reader that I believe the most fully developed personality is androgynous. Since I am writing here about female gods, I am emphasizing a man's response to the femaleness of woman and a woman's awareness of her own femaleness as it is reflected in the male's response. If I were

writing about male deities, I could readily reverse the terms, but then there already is a lot written about male deities.

21. Joseph Campbell, *The Mythic Image*. Princeton, N.J.: Princeton University Press, 1974, p. 217.

22. I am inclined to believe that Catholics are perhaps a little bit too anxious to be swept along by Jungian psychology, feeling that somehow or other Jung's obvious interest in religion makes possible a rapprochement between traditional Christianity and psychoanalysis. In principle, such a rapprochement may well be possible, though the elaborate and frequently obscure Jungian models are terribly difficult to follow, and are, I believe, unnecessary if one wishes to use the history of religion as part of one's theological method. More to the point, Jung is not in particularly good repute with psychoanalysts outside of the relatively small Jungian school; indeed, he is viewed skeptically by most analysts in the Freudian tradition, especially since the publication of the recent Freud-Jung letters. The Jungian models may be interesting and helpful, but the study of Jung is not at present, nor is it likely to be, a means of dialogue between Catholicism and psychoanalysis.

23. Neumann does not discuss Celtic goddesses, but since it is a special interest of mine, I shall. If one strives to get behind the historicized versions of the Christian monks, the Celtic counterparts would appear to be Morrigan the Virgo, Maeve the Spouse, Brigid the Mother, and Bahd the Destroyer. But the Celtic goddesses tended to switch roles. Morrigan became the wife of the "Dagda the Good God" (rather like the later "God the Father" of the Christians); and Maeve, the "frenzied" mate of each of the kings of Ireland, was frequently destructive. The Irish rivers were also goddesses (such as Sionna and Boann—Shannon and Boyne now) who played at various times different goddess roles. Brigid was the sun goddess. (The Brigid cross of the Christians is an ancient Indo-European sun symbol.) Her feast—Inbolc—was on the first of February, when the westerlies begin to bring Ireland its three months of spring. The goddess's shrine was at Kildare. Interestingly enough, the Christian Brigid also had her feast on February first, she wore the Brigid cross, and presided over a monastery at Kildare. In few countries have the pagan customs been so systematically adopted as in Christian Ireland.

24. It is sufficient here to insist that the method being laid out in this volume is not an attempt to revive modernism or to argue for a kind of universal *"religion perennis."* On the contrary, both positions I reject as errors which violate the assumptions of the present method. Christian religious experience, those different religious experiences occasioned by the same or similar things-become-symbols, ultimately all speak to the same fundamental human questions; and they are occasioned by the same fundamental human dynamisms. But they speak in different voices and give different answers. We may have had to hear some answers before we were prepared to hear others; some answers may be implicitly contained in others; but some may contradict others, and some may complement or fulfill others. They are all hints of explanations, "rumors of angels," to use Peter Bergers phrase. But different angels generate different rumors—and some rumors are much better than others.

My own guess is that God speaks to that which is most open, most generous, most joyous in our own hopes, expectations, and aspirations. When the Spirit speaks to our spirit he touches ever more deeply the resources and the longings of our personalities, and both challenges the resources and confirms the longings. If this is the case for the Christian, Jesus can be seen as God's best Word, which definitively confirms the most passionate and hopeful human longings and definitively challenges the most open and the most noble of human resources. Jesus does not so much tell us something that is completely new as he validates something which we had always (or for a long time) hoped but never dared to believe was possible

There are many problems with my "guess"—not so much with what it says as with what it does not say. Where, for example, does one fit into it the self-revelations of God in the Eastern religions, which seem not only to be different from the Word spoken in Jesus but contrary to that Word? Could the Word have been spoken in another cultural milieu besides that of Second Temple Judaism? What would it have sounded like then? Can it be translated into other and seemingly opposed milieus? How? What about angels whose "rumors" seem to have been monstrously misunderstood—the devouring death goddesses of India and Mexico, to take an example pertinent to the subject of his book? These are tough questions, but I cannot address myself to them here.

25. The pagan probably would have been sophisticated enough in his more serious moments to distinguish between the goddess he was honoring and whatever was ultimate and absolute in the universe. The goddesses, then, were no more identified with the One than Mary is identified with the Trinity in Christian thought. In popular devotions, of course, there was much more confusion in both paganism and Christianity. To concentrate on the confusion and ignore, as it is to be feared many of the reformers did, the sacramental and revelatory nature of a feminine sacred person is to miss the point altogether.

Chapter 4

1. Walter Harrelson, *From Fertility Cult to Worship*, New York: Doubleday & Co., 1969.

2. Ibid., pp. 13–14.

3. *The Jerusalem Bible*, Garden City, N.Y.: Doubleday & Co., 1966.

4. *Dictionary of the Bible*, ed., John McKenzie, New York: Bruce Publishing Co., p. 903.

5. McHugh, *The Mother of Jesus*. Part I, pp. 101–156.

6. Raymond E. Brown, *The Gospel According to John*, New York: Doubleday & Co., Anchor Bible Series, 1966, pp. 101–111, 922–927. One should also consult Brown's extremely careful, cautious, and responsible *The Virginal Conception and Bodily Resurrection of Jesus*,

7. Max Thurian *Mary Mother of All Christians*, p. 16.

8. McHugh, *Mother of Jesus*, p. 52.

9. Raymond E. Brown, *The Gospel According to John I–XII*, p. 109.

10. Ibid., XIII–XXXI, p. 926.

11. Ibid., I–XII, p. 109.

12. Raymond E. Brown, *The Virginal Conception*, p. 132.

13. Ibid., p. 132.

14. Raymond E. Brown, "The Problem of the Virginal Conception of Jesus," *Theological Studies* 33, 1 (March 1972), p. 7.

Chapter 5

1. I hereby reject all charges of implying that fathers should be absolved from responsibility for taking care of an infant child. On the contrary, I think the peculiar notion that fathers should be free from such responsibility represents an injustice to both the father and the child. Still, I think few would disagree that psychologically, all other things being equal, the mother's relationship with an infant is more intimate than the father's. The father did not carry the child within his body for nine months and is not biologically designed for infant feeding. (I say "all things being equal," because we know situations in which the mother cares very little for the child and the father assumes the role of both father and mother.

2. There is also a paternal role in all human relationships in which the strong, vigorous, aggressive aspects of the human personality should emerge and be reciprocated. A man may find it easy to "father" his wife, but she has been forced to let the masculine part of her androgynous personality atrophy and may be quite incapable of "fathering" her husband. Again, the lack of symmetry can disturb the equilibrium of the relationship.

3. The dreams that many of us have of jumping into a large body of water are supposed to represent a desire to return to the secure, comfortable, all protected water environment of the womb. Of course, one should not exclude the possibility that sometimes we dream about jumping into water because we like to swim. As Freud himself remarked, sometimes a cigar is a cigar.

4. Neumann, p. 84. Text translated from Preuss, *Die Eingeborenen Amerikas*, p. 39.

5. Ibid., p. 131.

6. David Tracy points out to me that even theological terms are in fact limit-language.

7. I am convinced that if we wish to understand the power of the Mary myth, we must look to poetry and art, and to neither theology nor the desiccated popular devotion of recent times. I would have liked to include more pictures in this book, not as illustrations but as data for religious reflection. Unfortunately, the costs of book publication are such that more plates could not be included. Perhaps there will be a "coffee table" edition of this book. I hope, however, that the reader who is trying to follow my argument will dig out a book of Mary paintings from his local library and reflect upon them, as they illustrate the symbol we are trying to explore.

8. Francis Thompson, "Ode to the Setting Sun."

Chapter 6

1. At least among Irish Catholics after the Famine. Professor Emmet Larkin has noted that pre-Famine Irish Catholicism was something else altogether—less devout, perhaps, but also much less inhibited.

2. Gabriel Fielding, *Gentlemen in Their Season*, New York: William Morrow, 1966.

3. Lest I be inundated by outraged feminist ideologues, let me hasten to add that in a good marriage the husband plays exactly comparable roles for his wife.

4. Neumann, pp. 283–294.

5. Ibid., p. 317.

6. Ibid., p. 331.

7. I think Neumann is on less solid ground when he sees a similarity between representations of St. Anne with the Virgin and Child with the pagan mother-daughter-child paintings of Demeter, Kore, and the divine son, p. 332.

8. I would not suggest that one never revokes a commitment, never leaves a career or a vocation, or never changes one's mind. I merely assert that the limit-experience of spiritual transformation can be a growth-producing, illumination-bestowing event at the time when one is in a crisis of decision.

9. See my book, *Love and Play*, Chicago: Thomas More Association, 1975.

10. I have deliberately chosen to steer away from discussion of the controversial titles and doctrines of Mary because I think such discussion would distract from the purpose I have in mind. Nonetheless, both the doctrines of the Immaculate Conception and the Assumption are theological reflections on the image of the renewing, transforming virgin mother full of grace. They are both ways of saying that when Jesus was born into the world, humankind got a fresh new start; humanity began all over again. The whole earth was renewed, and in that renewal there comes potential for renewal for each of us. Like all religious doctrines, these two are exercises in limit-language, and as such they should be interpreted by the rules of language appropriate to this particular style of discourse.

Chapter 7

1. Presumably the women of the returning men had more or less the same reactions. Indeed, it has been argued that given the physiological capacity of women to have multiple orgasms, they may actually have been more sexually insatiable than their men in the archaic communities. One of the reasons for sexual restrictions and taboos and for the oppression of women may well have been that the destructive power of insatiable sexual hunger once awakened in women was more threatening to the tribe than male sexual passion. I am somewhat skeptical about this particular speculation, but I have no doubt that in archaic societies, men and women both understood the strength of the sexual urge and hence could not help but see it as sacred.

2. Lovemaking itself can be a limit-experience, though obviously it need not be, and presumably in most instances it is not, save perhaps in a very faint and small way.

3. Herbert Richardson, *Nun, Witch and Playmate,* New York: Harper & Row, Inc., 1971.

Chapter 8

1. Neumann, p. 147.

2. Ibid., p. 148.

3. Ibid., p. 149.

4. Ibid., p. 149.

5. Ibid.